Indian Economy

Trends and Challenges

Indian Economy
Trends and Challenges

Edited by
D. P. Tripathi

Chairman
Vichar Nyas Foundation
New Delhi

Vij Books India Pvt Ltd
New Delhi (India)

Published   by

Vij Books India Pvt Ltd
(Publishers, Distributors & Importers)
2/19, Ansari Road, Darya Ganj
New Delhi - 110002
Phones: 91-11-43596460, 91-11- 47340674
Fax: 91-11-47340674
e-mail : vijbooks@rediffmail.com
web: www.vijbooks.com

CONTENTS

Introduction

Political democracy in India has not been followed by economic democracy. This is not to deny the growth that India has registered over the last 63 years; especially over the last two decades, India has been growing at rates fairly higher than the world average. The Gross National Product (GNP) of India in fact has been twice the world average in recent years. From an economy impaired by an exploitative colonial past, India has emerged as a major economic power - the economy which was just a few billion dollars worth in 1990 is now worth more than a trillion dollars. Foreign exchange reserves are in the region of 275 billion dollars, which brings the comfort that any exigency created by shortage can be immediately surmounted through imports. The economy of India is the eleventh largest in the world by nominal Gross Domestic Product (GDP) and the fourth largest by purchasing power parity (PPP)(World Economic Outlook Database, April 2010, IMF). If the growth trend of the economy continues at 7-8 percent on compounded basis, our economy will multiply to double its present size in 10 years. According to the BRIC* Report, published by Goldman Sachs, India will be the second largest economy after China, by 2043.

However, all these encomiums lose their shine when we juxtapose them with the prevalent poverty, unemployment, levels of malnourishment and the sheer misery of the majority of the population. India continues to have anywhere between one-third and one-fourth of its population living in absolute poverty. Their number has declined very slowly, which leaves some 303 million people still in utter misery. Nearly half of India's children under six years of age are underweight and malnourished, nearly 80 percent suffer from anaemia while some 40 percent of Indian adults suffer from chronic energy deficit. Destitution and perpetual hunger kill and cripple thousands. The problem is more acute in rural India and among small

*BRIC - Brazil, Russia, India, China

children, pregnant women, dalits and adivasis (SCs & STs), especially in poorer states. Sayeda Hameed, Member, Planning Commission, in her article 'Planning for Malnourished Child', which follows this editorial, writes: "… I was appalled and overawed to confront the reality that we in India had the largest number of malnourished children in the world. Our figures were worse than Sub-Saharan Africa."

How has such a paradoxical growth, which is growth with partial development come about? What has caused such a split in the welfare of people, where a minority enjoys world class life-style but the majority survives in deep misery? Nearly three-fourth of the Indian population earns less than Rs.20 per day. Is it a case of misplaced priorities or some intractable structural problems that have not been adequately addressed? The answer lies with the latter which is, the growth strategy has never been explicitly employment-oriented. It was presumed that the planned growth strategy led by the public sector and with support to and control over the private sector would create a sound economic and social infrastructure and diversified industrial base, and the process would unleash employment which through multiplier effect would lead to manifold increase in employment as the economy would grow in upward spiral to higher and higher levels. But this did not happen, neither in the pre-reform regulated regime nor in the post-reform liberalised industrial and trade regime.

The reasons are not difficult to find. The stimulus to growth during the early post-independence years came from the State itself. It sought to expand the market through its capital and current expenditures and supported the private sector by investing in crucial infrastructural sectors and channelising household savings to finance private investment through the creation of a number of industrial development banks. The strategy did pay dividends during the decade-and-a-half immediately following Independence when rates of industrial growth were creditable by the international standards. But this growth through investment in heavy machinery and capital-intensive sectors happened at the cost of labour-intensive activities, i.e. growth was not accompanied by a corresponding growth in employment.

Private sector on its part could not compensate for this lack in the growth of employment. Industrial licensing and import licensing, the twin measures infamously known as License-Permit Raj, were brought into operation to regulate private sector activity in conformity with the government priorities and to direct scarce resources to industries considered important. However, the system created a culture of rent seeking, erected barriers to entry and exit, provided indiscriminate and indefinite protection to private industrial class from both domestic and foreign competition, and led to misallocation of resources. Another factor that affected the growth of the manufacturing sector was excessive protection to small scale enterprises. Once a product was classified to be produced by the small scale sector no further capacity was permitted for medium or large scale units, though they were allowed to produce. All further expansion and capacity creation was reserved only for the small scale sector. This prevented the medium and large scale units to operate at optimal size and to achieve economies of scale. As a result both the industrial expansion and the employment thereof from the private sector could not come about with the magnitude that had been envisioned.

This rather low level of employment in the industrial sector along with massive unemployment in rural areas, which continues to be home to majority of the population, resulted in a very low purchasing capacity in the economy which in turn restricted the expansion of market for mass consumption goods. Also, war with China in 1962 and with Pakistan in 1965 and 1971, a flood of refugees from East Pakistan in 1971, droughts in 1965, 1966, 1971, and 1972, and the first world oil crisis in 1973-1974, all jolted the economy and undermined the ability of the State to provide stimulus to growth. As a consequence, growth decelerated throughout the seventies, making a severe dent on the employment situation in India.

In order to come out of this growth impasse, a series of policy changes were carried out, liberalising the highly regulated economy and making production for exports, rather than for internal market, more profitable. The first phase of this new liberal economic policy was introduced in 1978-80. However, the rise in the cost of petroleum in the world market forced the government to revert to a more regulated economy.

The second phase of economic liberalisation was carried out during the early months of Rajiv Gandhi's premiership (1985-1989). Compared with the low economic growth rate of the 1970s (with an average annual GDP growth rate of 3.5 percent), the 1980s witnessed moderate to high growth, with an average annual GDP growth rate of 5.5 percent. The modest liberalisation of the import regime facilitated access to new technologies, which, in turn, encouraged expansion in the consumer durables, electronics and petrochemicals industries. This increase in the rate of growth, however, was achieved through excessive borrowing by the government, both from domestic and international markets.

Given the high accumulation of debt and the concomitant burden of debt servicing, and in the absence of an adequate growth in exports, India found itself unable to withstand the adverse effects of the Gulf crisis in the mid-1990s. Partly on account of this and partly on account of the poor political assessments of credit-rating agencies, which believed that a minority Government would be unable to pursue policies that would stabilise the Indian economy, India's credit rating began to slip in the latter half of 1990s. Faced with the risk of default, the government reverted back to stiff import control measures, borrowed extensively from the IMF and, in July 1991, devalued the rupee by 20 percent.

The balance-of-payments crisis of mid-1991 coincided with the arrival in office of a new Congress Party government, led by Prime Minister P. V. Narasimha Rao, with Dr. Manmohan Singh as Minister of Finance. The Rao-Singh team utilised the opportunity opened by the payments crisis to make the Indian economy more accessible to foreign trade and investment flows. Implementing a traditional structural adjustment programme designed with the assistance of the World Bank and the IMF, India liberalised its trade and investment policies, hin a announced a programme of fiscal stabilisation aimed at reducing the fiscal deficit from more than 8.5 percent of GDP to 5 percent, initiated a policy for phasing out short-term external debt exposure and reduced the current-account deficit from more than 3 percent of GDP to less than 2 percent within a year. Along with this medium-term adjustment and stabilisation programme, the Government gradually introduced extensive changes in industrial and tax policies.

The policies to transform the Indian economy from an inward-oriented, import-substituting model of industrial development to an outward-oriented model were further developed by successive governments, throughout the 1990s. As a result, the policies not only prevented external default, but also helped to increase India's foreign-exchange assets several-fold within a short period of time. There was a sharp decrease in both fiscal and current-account deficits and an improvement in the external debt profile. The rise in reserves in the mid-1990s coincided with India's opening of its stock market to investment by foreign institutional investors, such as pension and mutual funds. India's recovery from a balance-of-payments crisis is regarded as one of the fastest achieved under an IMF-World Bank adjustment and stabilisation programme. In part, the success of the Indian strategy lay in the ability of the authorities to ensure relative freedom from the IMF-World Bank orthodoxy, in order to pursue an unorthodox and unconventional approach to fiscal and balance-of-payments correction. As well as stabilising the economy, these policies also helped to accelerate the rate of growth of the Indian economy. Compared with the long-term annual rate of growth of around 4 percent during 1950-90, the Indian economy was able to register an average rate of growth of more than 5.7 percent per year in the period 1992-2008, with annual growth averaging 8.8 percent in 2003-08.

Here, it would be instructive to find out how employment grew during this period of structural transformation and the consequent moderate, impressive and very impressive growth of the economy. The truth is total employment in the public sector between the period 1991-2006 actually came down from 190.58 lakh persons to 181.88 lakh persons. The employment in private sector though grew from 76.77 lakh persons in 1991 to 87.71 lakh persons in 2006, the addition was of only 11 lakh persons over a period of 15 years. An impressive growth accompanied by a shortfall in the level of employment in the public sector and a minuscule growth in employment in the private sector in an economy so abundant in labour force simply implies that economic benefits had been distributed unequally and inequalities had grown.

Amit Bhaduri, the renowned economist and an academic par excellence, sums up this growth phenomenon succinctly in his incisive article 'Predatory Growth' which we have published in this issue of Think

India (pp.26-36). He argues that "India is experiencing a growth rate of some 7-8 percent in recent years, but the growth in regular employment has hardly exceeded 1 percent. This means most of the growth, some 5-6 percent of the Gross Domestic Product (GDP), is the result, not of employment expansion but of higher output per worker. This high growth of output has its source in a rise in labour productivity. According to official statistics, between 1991 and 2004, employment fell in the organised public sector, and the organised private sector hardly compensated for the shortfall. In the corporate sector and in some organised industries, productivity growth comes from mechanisation and longer hours of work. Edward Luce of the Financial Times (London) reported that the Tata's Jamshedpur steel plant employed 85,000 workers in1991, to produce one million tonnes of steel worth US$ 0.8 million. In 2005, production rose to five million tonnes, worth about US$ 5 million, while employment fell to 44,000. In short, output increased approximately by a factor of five and employment dropped by a factor of one half, implying an increase in labour productivity by a factor of ten. Stephen Roach, chief economist of Morgan Stanley, reports a similar case with the Bajaj motorcycle factory in Pune. In the mid-1990s, the factory employed 24,000 workers to produce one million two-wheeler units. In 2004, aided by Japanese robotics and Indian information technology, 10,500 workers produced 2.4 million units, that is, an increase in labour productivity by a factor of nearly six with less than half the labour force more than doubling the output. One could multiply such examples, but this is broadly the name of the game everywhere in the private corporate sector.

The manifold increase in labour productivity without a corresponding increase in wages and salaries becomes an enormous source of profit and also a source of international price competitiveness in a globalising world. Nevertheless, this is not the entire story, perhaps not even the most important part of the story. The whole organised sector, to which the corporate sector belongs, accounts for less than a tenth of the labour force. Simply by the arithmetic of weighted averages, a 5-6 percent annual growth in labour productivity in the entire economy is possible only if the unorganised sector, accounting for the remaining 90 percent of the labour force, also contributes to this growth. Direct information is not available on this count, but several micro-studies and surveys show the broad pattern. Growth of labour productivity in the unorganised sector, which includes most of agriculture, comes from lengthening working hours to a significant extent as this sector has neither labour law worth the name nor social security protection. Subcontracting to the unorganised sector along with casualisation of labour on a large scale become convenient devices to ensure longer working hours without higher pay. Self-employed workers, totalling 260 million, expanded fastest during the high-growth regime, providing an invisible source of labour productivity growth. Ruthless self-exploitation by many of these workers in a desperate attempt to survive, keeps them putting in long hours of work, with very little extra earning and adds both to productivity growth contributing directly and indirectly, through various forms of formal and informal subcontracting, to corporate profit, and to human misery.

One may recall some of the major employment policies that have been operated from time to time. These are: some budget-supported public works programmes, lately supplemented by a demand-driven income supplementation programme for the rural families, some, mainly bank and other financial institutions supported, micro-level productive asset-creation programmes along with certain measures to improve the supply side capabilities and information and placement channels in order to equip the labour force and help it find and retain employment, including some laws to protect and promote the interests of the workers vis-a-vis the stronger bargaining power of the large corporate employers. The need for such protective steps for the labour force is apparent from the ground level fact that the corporate sector is not too favourably inclined to give employment its due role, for despite enjoying internationally the comparative advantage of rather low rates of wages and operating in a capital-scarce economy, the corporate sector is spending as low as 8 percent of the total cost of production by way of its wage bill. With such low contribution to employment and the increasing practice to go in for informal mode of employment adopted by the private companies, any encouragement to them by means of public policies is fraught with prospects of being counter productive.

There are also the problems of sectoral disparities. This growth activity has remained concentrated, mostly in the service sector and the manufacturing sector, but the agricultural sector, which still employs nearly three-fifths of the work-force, has seen a deceleration in its growth rate. This is reflected in the rural-urban divide, with the cities and towns showing an economic dynamism and rural India experiencing considerable economic difficulties. Yet another divide is apparent within the cities themselves, with the poor and marginalised (many of them migrants from the rural areas) being pushed to the outer fringes of the urban centres and being denied basic facilities, while the city centres and suburbs begin to mirror the more prosperous urban locations elsewhere in the world. All these disparities are expressed in a general unease that rapid growth has not been broadly based. There is an awareness across the political spectrum that uneven economic expansion is not sustainable.

In the light of such an uneven spread of the gains from rapid growth it has become apparent, at least internally, that focussing only on some areas of success and transformation does not provide a complete picture of the Indian economy today. The IT sector is growing in leaps and bounds, but, although it employs more than 20 lakh young men and women, this still constitutes just a small fraction of the Indian labour force of some 40 crore. A true transformation of the Indian economy will take place only when the manufacturing and agricultural sectors enjoy the same degree of success as the IT sector.

In the Parliamentary elections held in May 2009, the UPA Government was returned to power on the promise of promoting 'inclusive' growth. The mandate was seen as an endorsement of government policies, which over the previous five years had sought to combine rapid growth with a substantial increase in expenditure on welfare programmes. The latter was intended to reduce disparities and spread growth more evenly. Foremost among the welfare programmes was the National Rural Employment Guarantee Scheme (NRGS) which promised one member of every eligible household in the rural areas 100 days of employment in a public-works programme. Although, since its inauguration in 2005, this mammoth programme has not proved entirely successful, it has, nevertheless, made a difference to the poorest households in India's villages. On reassuming power in June 2009, the new Government reiterated its resolve to pursue inclusive growth. This would involve expanding programmes targeted at the deprived and vulnerable, in both rural and urban India while simultaneously restoring the growth momentum that had declined with the onset of the global recession.

The key to India sustaining her current high rates of growth lies in the economy and the polity's ability to promote broad-based, labour-intensive industrialisation. Economic growth must be seen as the outcome of employment growth. Our bench mark should be a time-bound programme for full employment. How much the growth in employment would contribute to growth in output depends on how productively labour can be employed. This requires a programme of decentralised, employment-intensive, rural industrialisation through participatory democracy at the local level. Work opportunities must be conceived by the communities through innovative plans aimed at fulfilling the basic needs. An efficient and participatory management of land, water and tree cover with human power can achieve this. This inclusive industrialisation would be characterised by labour-intensive technology, small scale production by the masses and maximum direct linkages between consumer and producer. This route to industrialisation would create a large range of goods and services for the local market, created through the purchasing power generated locally, in the hands of the poor. This is the route through which the poor, who have been bypassed by the industrialisation so far, would enter the larger economy with dignity, as both consumers and producers.

D. P. Tripathi

Syeda Hameed

Planning for Malnourished Children: Reed Cane of New Hope

Come; recognise that your imagination and reflection and sense-perception and apprehension are like the reed-cane on which children ride.

(Mathnawi of Mevlana Jalau'ddin Rumi)

There were over 200 people in the room. The largest contingent was of women who had come from 16 states representing the vibrant diversity of India. The states represented were Andhra Pradesh, Assam, Bihar, Chhattisgarh, Delhi, Himachal Pradesh, Jharkhand, Kerala, Madhya Pradesh, Maharashtra, Meghalaya, Orissa, Rajasthan, Tamil Nadu, Uttar Pradesh and West Bengal.

They were Anganwadi workers, ASHAs (Accredited Social Health Activists) Supervisors, Child Development Programme Officers, Auxiliary Nurse Midwives, Women SHG Members, Members of Panchayati Raj institutions - both women and men. Many had come to the capital for the first time. Rubbing shoulders with them were Ministers, Secretaries, senior bureaucrats, officials from PMO, Members of the PM's Nutrition Council, officials from other Commissions, such as National Commission for the Protection of Child Rights, National Institutions, experts in public health, nutrition, education, water, sanitation, rural development, medical professionals and representatives of voluntary agencies and community based organisations. There were District Collectors, medical officers and field workers. The event that had been organised on August 7 and 8, 2010 by the Planning Commission was a Multistakeholder Retreat on Addressing India's Nutrition Challenges.

Since 2004, when I was appointed as Member, Planning Commission, I have been confronted with an intractable problem. As someone with the sectoral responsibility for children, I was appalled and overawed to confront the reality that we, in India, had the largest number of malnourished children in the world. Our figures were worse than Sub Saharan Africa. For me as for many others, India's high growth rate lost its sheen when, despite all the resources allocated to it, malnutrition could not be handled and brought down, in any significant way. This development paradox haunted me and I hoped that we would find the answer to this together, as our strength lies in our collective wisdom, resolve and action.

The issue of malnutrition has many stakeholders. Everyone has views which are often difficult to reconcile. So, several meetings, consultations, seminars etc. are held, some technical 'solutions' repeatedly propounded, articles and learned papers are written and endless discourse goes on. But while "what" needs to be done is well accepted, the discourse does not really suggest "how" to make this happen. The 'how' is rooted in the reality of India's villages and has to be grounded there. While policies are debated and framed in a national and state capital, children continue to be born and their state of malnutrition continues, appallingly unabated. The clock ticks, the deprivation measurement numerals continue to notch up. My mind recalls and mulls over lines of Gabriela Mistral:

> Many things can wait, a child cannot
>
> Now is the time, her blood is being formed
>
> Her bones are being made and her mind developed
>
> To her we can't say tomorrow
>
> Her name is today.'

The people who had assembled on the first day of the Retreat at the Indian Council of Agricultural Research had undertaken to sit together and develop a common strategy to improve the nutritional status of children. For this, a common understanding and a shared vision needed to be built. It was expected to yield a renewed commitment and a consensus for moving forward.

The process had been set in motion earlier during the year by the Union Ministry of Women and Child Development by holding consultations with its counterpart State Ministers and Secretaries. The Ministry had also invited the Parliamentary Consultative Committee Members for a discussion on Malnutrition and held a consultation with young MPs. Their suggestions were taken on board in preparing the Ministry's strategy paper. A separate paper was prepared by the Ministry of Health. All these separate elements culminated in a joint paper on the subject which became the background document placed before the participants of the Retreat.

The Planning Commission's idea was to bring on one platform, voices from the entire spectrum of children's universe, especially voices from the field. These are voices which are often not heard; these are voices which touch the life of the child and reach the furthest village. It was around this idea that the workshop was conceptualised. Design and leadership teams were constituted as microcosms of the many stakeholders who would participate in the Retreat. This was done to ensure that the design and organisation of the Retreat responded to the different stakeholders' perspectives. The leadership team consisting of the political top brass gave the vision and guided the process, which was critical for its crystallization, multisectoral representation and effective impact.

The Retreat used Real Time Strategic Change methodologies such as listening to the voices of Stakeholders, small group dialogue, large group interaction, multi or open voting, preferred futuring and visualisation of participatory planning techniques. An exhibition of the state best practices, innovation, local materials and poster presentations by state teams facilitated interstate sharing and learning. Local folk media displays and street theatre in the evening session, enabled a shared appreciation of different issues and local solutions in different state contexts.

Voices from the field were slotted for hearing from the very start of the meeting. 'This is our first time' several women participants said; they had never stood before the microphone. For many it was their first visit to the capital. From Chomu tehsil of Jaipur district, Archana Jangid, an SHG member spoke about the importance of post partum care and feeding of mothers. The programme started by the Rajasthan Minister of WCD, Bina Kak, is called Kalewa. It ensures that women are kept two days after the delivery and fed warm, highly nutritious food, which is a wonderful support in the early initiation of breast feeding, colostrum feeding and better care of the new born. They are thus better equipped to return home, strong enough to look after themselves and their child. From Chhattisgarh, Karmi, a Sahiya (Accredited Social Health Activists[ASHAs] are called Sahiyas in Chhatisgarh) spoke of how she looks after adolescent girls. 'I ask them to eat green leafy vegetables and nutritious grains. And they try to follow my advice. But what do I get for all my work? For completing the cycle of immunization per child, I just get Rs 200. And for sterilization of women, I get merely Rs 150. Is that enough?' Her question lingered on in our minds, throughout the Retreat. Those who discussed the need to incentivise ASHAs, questioned whether incentivisation at the current level was sufficient!

From Palghar in Maharashtra, Chhaya Yadav, another ASHA, told us with pride that she does not allow her women to deliver babies at home. 'I explain to them that they will get money from the Janani Suraksha Yojana of Bharat Sarkar. As for the children, I never allow a child from my area to become malnourished. I work *saath saath* along with the Anganwadi worker. But do we get enough payment for taking women to the hospital? Everything costs a lot, even taking a rickshaw. We women are role models for other women who want to enlist as ASHAs. But when they see what we get, they hesitate.' Chhaya's dream is to become an ANM - and as her voice resonated in the room, I saw a flicker of hope in the eyes of other ASHAs.

A man then spoke up, breaking into what was so far a "women only" discourse. Sachin Baghel is Member of the Rajnandgaon Zila Parishad in Chhattisgarh. "To speak the truth, I did not even know what malnutrition was. But ever since I learnt of it, I feel that we in Panchayats should be involved. It will yield results, I guarantee. Please take us into confidence." He then described the Village Health and Nutrition Day in his area. His pride was visible. And as he spoke, an idea began to form in the mind of some listeners. How can we work towards malnutrition - free panchayats? How can other members, like Mumtaz, a Block Panchayat Member in Mallepuram, Kerala, become change leaders, leading a societal campaign against malnutrition?

Aruna Sharma is an Asha-Sahyogini from Amer, in Rajasthan. She said that in her state, both the functions of ASHA and Saathin have been combined into one functionary. She complained of the difficulty children have, in travelling long distances for immunization. Also there was no provision for delivery in her PHC. She wanted a link with private hospitals and desired that AWW be given incentive payment in case they have to take women in, for private delivery. As she spoke of health and nutrition of women and children, it seemed as if there was no dividing line between the sectors or the programmes. What mattered to her, was ensuring that the mother and child were healthy, nourished and the child had every opportunity for realising her development potential. Ashima from Uttar Dinajpur in West Bengal said there was no infrastructure for Anganwadis. For instance, there was no *pucca* building, *bijli*, running water, hygiene etc. There was no convergence between WCD workers and Health workers. She asked for the involvement of PRIs and that special fund for nutrition is placed with the Pradhan, to promote local initiatives and locally appropriate feeding and care. The food (SNP) given in her project was inadequate, both in quality and quantity. In remote areas, in any case, there was hardly any access. She argued for increasing the per unit cost of supplementary food, provided in AWCs.

Spontaneous voices of field functionaries kept placing their experiences before a rapt audience. From Raygadha, Orissa, B Kamalangi, the ICDS Supervisor spoke. She said that locally available nutritious cereal was used by mothers and self help groups. This made a difference and could be replicated elsewhere. Gajapati's problems were lack of participation from the women and PRI. There was also the problem of birth spacing and numbers of children. Health and WCD moved on two separate tracks. Water, sanitation and hygiene followed their own course. Nothing reached the Naxal affected areas. She pleaded for nutrition to be placed on everyone's agenda. 'You need to address exclusion, develop special plans for Naxal areas, and involve people and Panchayats'.

Manasi Roy, ASHA from Malda, West Bengal, spoke of the challenge of looking after children under two. Her experience pointed that the best option was home contact. She insisted that the most effective way was for the Anganwadi Worker to make home visits to ensure that pregnant women went for regular antenatal care check ups, were given nutrition counselling and were encouraged to have institutional deliveries. It would also promote better neonatal care, and encourage early and exclusive breast feeding for the first six months of life, with complementary feeding after six months, along with continued breastfeeding for two years or beyond.

Mukesh, a Gram Sevak from Jaipur, spoke about the need to focus on what he termed, 'Minus 9 months (in uterus) to plus 2 year old babies.' In his Panchayat, he found that commitment of Members was growing. Panchayats, therefore, should never be left out. Programmes should be sent up from lower levels to the district. He wanted a constituency to be developed around Malnutrition. Villagers, he said, want to participate, so they should be enabled to do so through some common forum or village committee. He was emphatic about the need for better monitoring and making malnutrition visible on wall charts/maps in the panchayat ghar.

P Amuda, a firebrand District Collector from Tamil Nadu, described how she was able to bring better results in her district, Dharmapuri. With lowest indicators of all TN districts, it is the most backward and problematic district in the state. She attributed her success partly to better payment made to the workers. TN gives Rs.5000 to the AWW and Rs.3000 to the AWH plus a pension provision is kept for both. A couple of months ago I had seen for myself, the success of her efforts. I had visited Anganwadis in Dharmapuri and seen the Anganwadi worker preparing food, teaching the kids, testing the salt for iodine with little kits, supplied by UNICEF. I had seen children playing and making puzzles. This was in sharp contrast to the Anganwadis I had been seeing across the country in the last 5 years - a handful of crying and dirty looking children sitting in dank rooms, just waiting for a bowl of barely edible food. For a Collector with a conscience for children's shows, how much difference can really be made by a little bit of extra effort and by supporting the field functionaries? Usha Rani, an AWW from TN said that being an AWW, along with so many AWWs from different states, is like being a part of a large family. She suggested a second AWW, so that both the under 3s and the 3-6 year olds are better cared for. As she explained her experience in the state and how the situation of children had improved, participants saw the wisdom of her suggestions. Even the sceptics understood the need for a nutrition counsellor or additional AWW to reach the mother and more vulnerable younger child in the family.

All the participants were asked to form 16 groups of 10 members each, ranging from the highest government officials to grass root workers. They were asked to list three things (within the context) which made them glad, three, which made them sad and three, which made them mad. The lists would be tallied by the group and narrowed to the three highest 'glads', 'sads' and 'mads'. A master tally of all groups would then come up with the 3 top 'glads', 'sads' and 'mads'. On the glad side, the highest score went to the Immunization Programme, the second place went to the general awareness created about children and mothers because of the Anganwadi programme and the third was the acceptance of the ICDS scheme across the country. They were saddest because of the communication gap between the AWW and the higher district officials, which undermines her work, second that the value of AWW has not been recognised or adequately compensated and third, the lack of water supply, toilets and connectivity in the centres. Finally, they were mad because of the poor quality infrastructure of AWC. Not only were the centres unusable and broken down but the furniture and other items were of cheapest quality. They were also mad because communication and travel within their area was impossible without cycles or mopeds.

This exercise was a beautiful way of revealing the commonality among AWWs from different corners of the country. It also created an affinity amongst those who heard and shared each other's joy and pain. This affinity enabled all the different groups of people in the room, to come together, with a common vision and a commitment to collective action.

A framework for a Multisectoral National Plan of Action to reduce and prevent Malnutrition, especially of mother and child was the final outcome of the two days. Certain common understandings were achieved because of which recommendations could be framed. All present, endorsed the recommendations and renewed their commitment to act on them, within specific time frames. There was general consensus on the way to move forward.

A common understanding emerged on what needs to be done and how. In terms of what needs to be done, a few essentials were named.

Household food security and livelihood, women and child care, health care, water, environment and hygiene, infant and young child care and feeding practice, developing capacities of workers, influencing community practices, and continued surveillance. The discussion focussed on how all this would be done - what options existed, how institutional mechanisms could be used and how communities could be empowered, to make it happen.

Some principles for action were agreed upon and articulated. Highest attention was centred on the adolescent girl, pregnant woman, breastfeeding mother and children under two years; thus preventing under nutrition as early as possible, across the life cycle. It was suggested that the Anganwadi Centre should equally focus on its surrounding area, that all programmes be converged at the level of the village, that women should be at the core, as agents of social change, and services should be universalised and interventions should be multisectoral. There should be safeguards against conflict of interest and good governance, with accountability, should be ensured.

A new National Child Malnutrition Prevention and Reduction Programme should be initiated in the most vulnerable districts and states, facing the largest challenge of addressing high levels of undernutrition and related mortality. This should be in a mission mode with convergence of schemes such as NRHM, ICDS, Rajiv Gandhi Scheme for Adolescent Girls, Indira Gandhi Matritva Sahyog Yojana, Total Sanitation Campaign, National Rural Drinking Water Programme (NRDWP), Midday Meals, MG National Rural Employment Guarantee, PDS, and the proposed National Food Security Act Scheme. This would ensure that all the determinants of health and nutrition work together. An important aspect would be concentration on the adolescent girl, the pregnant woman plus children under two years of age.

Everyone was agreed upon the essential component of training. Kunti Bora, Supervisor, Kokodonga ICDS Centre, District Golaghat, Assam summarised it best, by quoting from Rabindranath Tagore 'Do not give me a fish but instead, teach me how to catch a fish.'

As Kunti, Mumtaz, Archana, Sachin and Usha led discussions in different groups, their animated dialogue was reflected on flip charts. Excitement filled the air when "the multivoting bindi exercise" started. Strategy options that emerged from group work were being voted for, prioritised, and endorsed or modified or rejected. And as people crowded around the charts to see which charts have the most "bindis", a quiet feeling of satisfaction filled the air. B Kamalangi from Rayagadha said, "I had been hearing; now I am heard. The Workshop provided me an opportunity to share realities from the field. We spoke without fear and prejudice; there was no language barrier."

Each one present realised that together we could make a difference and that the change had begun, to start with, within ourselves. The roadmap we had prepared was the first step in addressing the development paradox that used to haunt me. I realised however that the process once started is not going to be a magic wand. Its progress will continue to be slow and laborious, but its outcomes will be seen in all Surveys; NFHS, DLHS, SRS. We all derive wisdom from the words of Jalau'ddin Rumi:

> Constant, slow movement teaches us to keep working
>
> Like a small creek that stays clear
>
> That doesn't stagnate but finds a way
>
> Through numerous details, deliberately.
>
> That is what gives us hope.

Prakash Karat

The Political Economy of Growth in India

The ruling establishment cites the high GDP growth rate as indicative of economic development and consequently the well-being of the people. GDP growth was 7.4 per cent in 2009-10 and this year it is expected to touch 8.5 per cent. It is true that the Indian economy did not suffer a deep downturn unlike most countries across the world, in 2008-09. But India could avoid the type of financial meltdown witnessed in the advanced countries, primarily because of the public sector dominance in India's financial sphere.

Skewed Growth

We have to examine closely what the political economy of growth means, for the country and the people. Earlier, when the neo-liberal policies were being put in place, it was propounded that GDP growth would trickle down to the people. But this has not happened.

There is no doubt that the Indian economy has a tremendous growth potential. But what are the politics and economics of such a pattern of growth?

Agrarian Crisis

The overall GDP growth figure conceals the skewed nature of the growth process under neo-liberalism. Agriculture grew by only 0.2 per cent in 2009-10, after a slow growth of 1.6 per cent in 2008-09. Foodgrains production fell by 7.5 per cent in 2009-10, over the last year. The decline in public investment in agriculture in the 1990s has contributed to the present stagnation in agriculture production and the agrarian crisis.

The thrust of the policies in agriculture is towards promoting greater corporate penetration and withdrawal of State support for the peasantry. The recommendations of the National Commission on Farmers have been shelved. Urea prices have been hiked with the ulterior aim of deregulating fertilizer prices and cutting down fertilizer subsidies drastically. Efforts are on to enact the Seed Bill, which will facilitate greater control of the seed market by the MNCs. The US-India Agricultural Knowledge Initiative is the vehicle through which the interests of the MNCs are being pushed, making agricultural research in India, increasingly dependent on American technology and big capital.

Trade liberalisation in agriculture is being carried forward through FTAs (Free Trade Agreements) like the one signed with the ASEAN in January 2010 and the one currently being negotiated with the EU. These FTAs will lead to drastic reductions in tariffs on agricultural imports which will hurt the small peasant producers of cash crops, fruits and milk and fishermen. The entire gamut of policy initiatives in agriculture, marks a shift away from the limited measures undertaken by the UPA-I to support the peasantry at the behest of the Left parties, like increase in MSP for wheat and rice, loan waiver etc., and are directed towards promoting foreign and domestic corporate agri-businesses at the cost of peasant agriculture.

Poverty Perpetuated

With half the workforce in India allied to agriculture, the agrarian crisis has deleterious effects on much of the rural population. This has a direct bearing on rural poverty, halting thereby, progress in poverty alleviation. As far as rural poverty is concerned, the percentage of people not able to spend enough on food, to reach the 2400 calories daily intake (the official nutrition norm) rose from 75 per cent in 1993-94 to 87 per cent in 2004-05. Official poverty estimates are much lower and show a spurious decline because the 2400 calorie norm is not applied to calculate the poverty line. The high GDP growth rate has had no impact on hunger and malnutrition.

Food Inflation

The unprecedented food price inflation is a result of the policies being pursued. The curtailment of the public distribution system with introduction of the targeted system; the acceptance of the market as the arbiter in trading and distribution of food items, exemplified by the forward trading system and the refusal to have a universal public distribution system which is seen as inimical to market values, have all contributed to food inflation. Speculative future trading in essential commodities like wheat, chana dal, potato etc. which was earlier banned due to opposition from the Left parties, has been lifted. These have contributed to a political economy which perpetuates deprivation and hunger. All talk of "inclusive growth" becomes a chimera when the right to food and access to food is restricted and denied.

The failure to rein in inflation can also be traced to government policies. The hike in indirect taxes on petro-products in the Union Budget 2010 and the second round of fuel price increase in June as per the Kirit Parikh Committee recommendations to deregulate fuel prices, have further stoked all round inflation.

Fiscal Policies: Benefits Rich

The government policies are designed to help big businessmen and the corporates to make super profits and to enable the transfer of resources to the rich and the powerful. Indirect taxes are being sharply raised, which burden the people. The budget provided for Rs.60,000 crore to be raised through increases in indirect taxes. At the same time, additional direct tax relief of Rs.26,000 crore was doled out to the corporates and the affluent sections. In the previous year 2009-10, corporate tax concessions worth Rs.80,000 crore, were given away. The Direct Taxes Code proposed by the government, brings down the rates of corporate tax, wealth tax and income tax on the upper brackets.

As a result of all these, the Central tax-GDP ratio, which had gone up to 12 per cent in 2007-08, due to the pressure of Left parties, to mobilise resources for welfare spending have come down to 10.4 per cent in 2009-10.

Dictate of International Finance Capital

International finance dictates the agenda of economic reforms. Despite the grim lessons of the global financial crisis, full convertibility on the capital account is still sought for. The push for FDI in retail trade is patently against the interests of the people and will kill employment on a large-scale in the retail trade. Yet, the government pursues this agenda.

Loot of Resources

Finally, the pursuit of GDP growth under neo-liberal policies is leading to enormous growth of capital and concentration of assets in the hands of narrow strata of the society. The number of 'dollar billionaires' in India has grown from 4 in 2001 to 49 this year. There is a sort of primitive accumulation of capital being promoted, which is marked by the plunder of natural resources like minerals. The unbridled loot of mineral resources through indiscriminate and illegal mining reveals the rapacious and predatory nature of neo-liberal capitalism. It is estimated that Rs.60,000 crore was made out of illegal mining and exports in Karnataka alone in the past year. Similarly, in Orissa, the illegal mining scam amounted to Rs.14,000 crore.

This is not an aberration under the present neo-liberal dispensation. The accumulation of capital is facilitated and accompanied by large-scale siphoning off of public funds, illegal extraction of mineral and natural resources and large-scale evasion of taxes.

Corrupt Nexus

The neo-liberal economic policies have spawned the nexus between big businessmen, politicians and bureaucrats. Its impact is being directly felt on the political system through the perversion of democracy and the pollution of politics. Big money and its agents are today ensconced within different layers of the political system. Public policy making is getting suborned by these forces.

Employment

An important feature of the economic growth has been the development of the IT sector and its significant contributions to exports. The growth of the IT sector has created jobs for the middle classes, but it has a limited impact on the overall scenario of large-scale unemployment. India's growth process is being driven primarily by the services sector. While the share of the industrial sector in GDP remains unchanged, the service sector's share in GDP is increasing at the cost of agriculture. Bulk of the employment in the services sector continues to remain in the unorganised sector in various forms of petty and informal activities, where productivity and earnings are extremely low and unstable. The services sector contributes 50 per cent of the GDP but only 25 per cent of employment.

It is in this vast informal sector that people are getting irregular employment and are being underpaid. It is mainly about this sector, that the National Commission for Enterprises in the Unorganised Sector Report stated that 77 per cent of this population spends less than Rs.20 per day or Rs.600 per month. Neo-liberal growth is unable to solve the problem of both urban and rural unemployment.

The growth process under the neo-liberal regime is only capable of generating very limited, formal job opportunities, for a handful in the organised sector, even as the masses are pushed into the swamp of the informal sector and forced self-employment, to live a life of insecurity and impoverishment. The government is trying to sell the slogan of "inclusive growth" to this section by redistributing a small part of the surpluses/ profits through half-hearted welfare programmes, even as the neo-liberal regime remains undisturbed. These are the sections of people bearing the brunt of the economic slowdown, job losses, agrarian distress and backbreaking food price inflation today.

Alternative Policies

There has to be an alternative to the present trajectory of high GDP growth sans equity and without development for the people. We can set out the contours of a set of such alternative policies.

- The first and foremost task is to tackle the agrarian crisis. Land reforms, instead of being reversed, have to be carried through to completion. Along with greater social expenditure in the rural areas, this is essential for widening the home market. Instead of moving towards corporatisation of agriculture, the farmers have to be assured of inputs at reasonable prices, so that agriculture can be sustainable. The goal of ensuring food security requires that farmers be given sufficient incentives to produce more.

- Adequate procurement and provision of a universal Public Distribution System is a must for a country like India, where hunger and malnutrition are unacceptably high.

- Public investment in agriculture and for developing the infrastructure must be stepped up, in a big way.

- Labour intensive industries for mass consumption goods should be promoted, so that more employment is created. Just like the Rural Employment Guarantee Scheme, an Urban Employment Guarantee Scheme should be introduced.

- The public sector should play the key role in the strategic sectors of the economy, including the financial sector. Speculative capital flows must be regulated and profits from such speculation should be taxed. Steps should be taken to recover the illegal money stashed away in tax havens and secret bank accounts, abroad.

- The system of direct taxes should be revised, so that capital gains tax is restored for stock market profits. The affluent should pay more taxes. The tax exemptions and concessions for them should be done away with. The increased revenue should go towards increased public expenditure in education and health. Education should get 6 per cent of the GDP and health at least 3 per cent.

To sum up, the economic growth registered under the neo-liberal dispensation cannot end poverty, hunger or unemployment. If the basic rights of the people to earn a decent livelihood and their right to health, education and well-being are to be ensured, then the present model of economic growth has to be changed. There has to be a departure from the neo-liberal framework and the alternative policies spelt out above, need to be put in place.

Yashwant Sinha

The Economic Policy of the NDA Government

When the Vajpayee government assumed office in March 1998, the country was faced with multiple challenges on the economic front. I was entrusted with the onerous task of reviving an economy which was in the doldrums once again. In the three years preceding 1997-98, the economy had registered a healthy growth rate of over 7 per cent of the GDP. However, on account of cyclical factors and lack of deft handling, this growth rate declined to less than 5 per cent in 1997-98. This huge deceleration in the economy was our first challenge. The second challenge was the economic crisis which was raging in our backyard, namely East Asia, which was putting pressure on our foreign exchange reserves also. As if these two factors were not challenges enough, the Prime Minister decided to conduct nuclear tests in May 1998. So, the budget for that year had to be prepared under the shadow of the economic sanctions which were imposed on India by the most powerful countries of the world, following these tests.

Our task, therefore, was three fold. First, we had to take steps to meet the current challenges which I have mentioned above. Second, we had to initiate long term policies to ensure growth with equity and third, we had to secure India's economic future. We had to take steps to secure the Indian economy by resolving its long standing and chronic problems.

The immediate task was to shore up India's depleting foreign exchange reserves. After the nuclear tests, the IMF option of a bail out on the balance of payments front, was not available. We, therefore, floated the Resurgent India Bonds which were sold to NRIs and PIOs, through the State Bank of India. This resulted in a net collection of US$ 4.25 billion. This was a major turning point and had an electrifying impact not only on India but all over the world. The powerful countries of the world realised that India will not bow down before them and ask for their mercy. A proud India will chart its own course, globally. The subsequent withdrawal of the economic sanctions was the result of this new found confidence in India.

On the long term policy front, we had to carry out the essential reforms in our economy, in order to ensure its orderly growth. We had to pay special attention to the agricultural and rural sector, the social sectors and the infrastructure sector, both physical and human, to ensure equitable growth.

We were convinced that there was a huge suppressed demand in India. In fact, the economic policies which had been followed for decades were clearly anti-consumer. The consumer had no choice and had to buy whatever was available in the market, irrespective of its quality and price. Monopolies were created in the public sector in the name of controlling the commanding heights of the economy. A favoured few in the private sector also enjoyed the benefits of monopoly. Competition, the driving force of the market, to ensure a better deal to the consumer, was totally at a discount. Entrepreneurship also became a casualty during the licence-permit-quota raj. So, along with unleashing consumer demand, we had to take steps to free the private sector from unnecessary controls and restrictions and allow their energy and talent free play. The public sector had to become lean, efficient and competitive.

Controlling inflation and moderating interest rate were necessary steps to encourage consumer demand. High inflation and high interest rates have been chronic problems of the Indian economy. They formed a vicious cycle and imposed an unacceptable burden on the economy. High interest rates were one of the reasons for the Indian economy being uncompetitive globally. Before we came into office, interest rates were as high as 18 to 20 per cent. High interest rates also made government borrowings extremely expensive. The interest burden of the government was going up steeply. We realised immediately that sooner rather than later, it would become unbearable.

Tackling inflation and softening interest rates, therefore, became an important objective of our policy. Since it spared for the consumer, the burden of high prices, it was a happy amalgam of good politics and good economics.

Given the sluggishness of the economy, we were looking for triggers to give it momentum and one of the triggers was housing and the construction sector.

Apart from the reduction in the rate of interest and income tax concessions, creation of a secondary mortgage market for the housing sector was also very important, which needed to be encouraged. This was the only step that could lead to the recycling of funds, by making mortgages tradable. To address this issue, we amended the National Housing Bank (NHB) Act so that a secondary mortgage market could come into existence. We studied the systems in vogue in other counties and incorporated those into the amendments to the Act. These steps led to a virtual explosion of house constructions. Banks and financial institutions vied with each other to advance loans, especially to the young for constructing or buying houses and apartments. This boom had its expected multiplier effect on the economy as a whole.

Moderating interest rates became a very important plank of our policy. In January 1999, we decided to reduce the interest rates on small savings from 14.5 per cent to 14 per cent. With falling inflation, the rates were successively reduced to 13.5 per cent in April 1999, to 12.5 per cent in April 2000 and then to 11 per cent in April 2001. In our budget of 2002 we not only reduced administered interest rates by another 0.5 per cent but also announced the bench marking of these rates to the average annual yields of government securities of equivalent maturities in the secondary market. The next year we reduced the rates further by 1 per cent. Thus, within a span of four years, the NDA government brought administered interest rates down from 14.5 per cent to 9.5 per cent, while at the same time fully protecting the real interest rate of the saver, by keeping inflation under control.

The government was the biggest borrower in the market and if it continued to pay high interest on its loans there was no way in which the overall interest rates could go down. Administered interest rates therefore had to be brought down in order to soften interest rates generally. But we were wrong in our thinking that we were combining good economics with good politics. The reduction in interest rates led to a lot of protests, especially from senior citizens and employees. Nobody was prepared to understand the concept of real interest rates. Nobody was willing to look at the falling inflation rate. They just looked at the loss in their interest income, and that was enough to turn them against the government. Arguments were also advanced that domestic savings would decline, since people would not be keen on saving because of the reduction in interest rates. On the contrary, history shows that domestic savings went up from 23.5 per cent to 29.7 per cent of GDP, during these years. This is a massive increase in domestic savings, despite the continuous reduction of interest rates, on all kinds of savings instruments.

The NDA government carried out deep and long lasting reforms in other sectors of the Indian economy also. The most important, of course, was a large number of reforms in the agricultural sector with a view to ensuring increase in both production and productivity of our agricultural produce. The Watershed Development Programme and the Kisan Credit Card scheme were meant to provide *paani* and *paisa* to the farmer, more easily and more adequately. Efforts were also made to unshackle the farmer from the bonds of various laws, at the state and central level, which handicapped him. In addition, there were reforms in the insurance sector, the banking sector, the capital markets sector, the electricity sector, the IT sector and the foreign investment sector. Fiscal reforms to control fiscal deficit, disinvestment to cut government's losses and strengthening the remaining public sector were important areas of our reforms programme.

Four chronic problems have bedevilled the Indian economy since Independence. It was the persistence of these four problems which made the Indian economy insecure, unstable, vulnerable to crises and dependent on foreign help. We can say with a reasonable degree of confidence that, at the end of the five years of NDA rule, these four chronic problems were effectively tackled and resolved for good.

The first of these was the problem of a precarious balance of payments. When we came into office, foreign exchange reserves stood at a little over $29 billion. On 3l May 2002, the reserves were almost $50 billion and growing. What is even more remarkable is that for the first time after twenty-three years, India recorded a current account surplus of 0.3 per cent of the GDP in 2001-02. The external debt-to-GDP ratio, signifying the extent of external debt vis-a-vis domestic output, declined from 24.3 per cent in end-March 1998 to 20.1 per cent at the end of September 2002. The debt-service-to-current-receipts ratio, which signifies the capacity of the country to meet its debt service obligation, improved from 19.5 per cent in 1997-98 to 13.8 per cent in 2001-02. Short-term debt also declined from $5.05 billion near end-March 1998 to $2.75 billion at end-March 2002.

In fact, our management of the external sector of the economy earned praise even from our erstwhile critics abroad and became a model for other developing countries.

The second chronic problem was perpetual food shortages and import of food grains. Through deft management of the food economy and procurement prices, it became possible for us to procure larger quantities of food grains from farmers, extend the area of procurement to other states, build large stocks of food grains in government godowns, launch food security schemes such as the Annapoorna and Antyodaya schemes and even emerge as one of the leading exporters of food grains, globally. We never even considered importing food grains to shore up our stocks as governments, immediately before and after us, have done.

The third chronic problem that we overcame was inflation. After the bitter onion and potato debate in the Parliament in 1990, we cannot recall a single occasion, when rising prices agitated MPs. Government figures show that the annual average WPI-based inflation, which was 10.6 per cent between 1991-92 and l 995-96, came down to 5.1 per cent between 1996-97 and 2000-01 and further to 4.1 per cent between 2001-02 and 2003-04.

The fourth chronic problem of the Indian economy is infrastructure. Vigorous measures were taken in all areas of infrastructure to develop world-class facilities. Telecom and highways are the more publicised success stories. But the achievements in the port sector where the average turnaround time dropped from 7.5 days in 1996-97 to 3.5 days in 2001-02, in housing where the target of twenty lakh houses a year was significantly exceeded, the financial sector reforms and reforms in the area of human resource development are no less impressive.

Most importantly, the Indian economy, which in the past, had been so prone to crisis, became safe and secure, not only for the present, not only temporarily, but for decades to come.

Suresh Neotia

Indian Economy: Promises and Challenges

Until about the 18th Century, India was a rich country, had a flourishing international trade, the people had enough food and abject poverty was nearly absent. The Western world, which was far behind India in terms of riches and advancement, began to grow with the invention of steam engine, which brought forth the industrial revolution. In the next 100 years, the Western world took a quantum leap and since then, they have been dominating the rest of the world.

The British occupation of India impaired the indigenous modes of production as they exploited the natural resources of India to feed their manufacturing base. They found a ready market in India, for their goods. A few of the British business houses, with the objective to strengthen the regime, set up engineering and jute industries. Engineering was meant to create the railway network so that the British could govern the whole country. Jute growers were exploited to provide cheap jute so that the final jute goods could be exported back into India, for consumption, at ridiculously low prices.

The first breakthrough in indigenous industry came at the end of the 19th Century and beginning of the 20th Century when Jamshedji Tata set up a steel plant, by bringing technology from America. G.D. Birla followed suit and set up cotton and jute mills, in spite of British resistance. These two great industrialists laid the foundation of industry in India.

Till independence, except for the houses of Tatas and Birlas and few others in Bombay, there was hardly any major industrial enterprise in Indian hands. Large volumes of capital, required to set up large-scale industrial enterprise, was not available. Nehru decided to set up industry - steel plants, engineering factories etc. - but kept it in the hands of public sector. Government control continued much after Nehru and the License Permit Raj was strengthened from the first term of Indira Gandhi. Only a handful of entrepreneurs could obtain such licenses; therefore until about 1990, a very limited growth in industry was achieved. There was no lack of Indian entrepreneurial skill but the paucity of capital due to high taxation and limited opportunity did not let it flourish. In the name of socialism, a stifling environment prevailed, with mild relaxation in the 1980s. It was only when Narasimha Rao became the Prime Minister, that Dr. Manmohan Singh as Finance Minister, started dismantling the rigid iron structure both on capital and licenses. A transformation took place within 5 years and Indian entrepreneurs responded to seize the opportunity and moved ahead to enlarge the industrial base. It was not only Dhirubhai Ambani who took the lead in dreaming big but there were many others, who joined the band-wagon to set up industry.

Rajiv Gandhi as the Prime Minister pushed computerisation though it was opposed by the Left and many others who suspected that it would lead to job losses. However, in spite of the stiff resistance, Rajiv Gandhi moved ahead with his programme and that is how the germs of a new revolution in Information Technology were laid in the 1980s. Instead of job losses, IT Industry created employment opportunities for tens of millions of the youth of the country. India was quick to grasp computerisation and a large industry gradually became dependent on the hardware and software for processing, manufacturing, accounting and systems. Today we find that even a small unit cannot function without the help and aid of computers. The second revolution came with the mass production of Maruti Cars, which provided an opportunity to millions of middle class consumers to own a vehicle. India graduated from rickety Ambassadors, Fiats cars and Bajaj scooters, to plentiful supply of four wheelers and two wheelers, by the year 2000.

The third revolution came with the adoption of mobile phone technology in India. Some of the companies, particularly Bharti, took the lead and made it into an instrument of mass communication. The entry of Reliance into mobile telephony, brought in stiff competition which brought the tariff down and mobile phones became affordable to the common man.

From a few thousand handsets, India has nearly 500 million connections today.

Cement was partially decontrolled in 1982. It brought in huge investment in the industry and the capacity from a mere 45 million tonnes per annum has grown to 250 million tonnes per annum today, in a span of just 15 years. Ambuja Cement took the major lead in cutting costs and branding the product. It converted cement from a commodity to a branded product. Other companies followed suit. The steel industry, which was earlier either with the Public Sector or with the Tatas, grew manifold - from a mere capacity of less than 10 million tonnes per annum, the industry took a quantum leap and today the capacity is close to 45 million tonnes per annum.

Entrepreneurial skill of India found an opportunity to manifest itself to become an object of envy around the world. Indians have gone beyond the shore and have purchased large enterprises in Europe, UK and USA. Today, in spite of the archaic bureaucratic system and political interference, the entrepreneurs in India have learnt to manage the system for the advancement of industrial growth in India.

To sum up, we must give credit to the three revolutions: first, the introduction of computers by Rajiv Gandhi, in his tenure as the Prime Minister, leading to the revolution in Information Technology; second, the mass production of affordable cars by Maruti and two wheelers led by Hero Honda and Bajaj; and third, the introduction of mobile phones, led by Bharti, that has enabled India to change its industrial horizon.

India is in a growth mode. From the year 2000, the economy has been growing at an average rate of 5 per cent, going up to 8 - 9 per cent, with one or two blip years. The economy which was just a few billion dollars in 1990, is now more than a trillion dollars worth. Foreign Exchange reserves are in the region of 275 billion dollars, which brings comfort that at any given time, if there is a shortage of any product, India can meet it by immediate import. There is an anxiety about the current account deficit in the economy which is at 6.5 per cent of GDP, much above the tolerable level. On the foreign exchange front, India continues to have a deficit, primarily because of substantial import of petroleum. The exports out of the country are steadily going up but they are not enough to meet the value of imports. Hence we have negative balance of trade.

If the growth trend continues at 7-8 per cent on compounded basis, our economy will multiply to double its present size in 10 years. However, the anxiety is that poverty continues to haunt more than 30 per cent of the population. A large section of the population continues to remain in a state of permanent hunger. On the other side, many Indians find their place among the richest in the world and the dichotomy is that the gap between haves and have-nots, continues to widen. Socially and politically, this means that a dangerous situation is building up. The income level at the bottom of the pyramid has to move up fast enough for India to move forward with confidence and pride. If India is to grow into an industrial giant, the infrastructure of roads, ports and power have to be addressed with great urgency. Though the government has accorded utmost priority to the issue, its implementation remains tardy. The speed with which it is being implemented, will take a long time before the infrastructure can facilitate the industry to grow faster.

India's entrepreneurial skill is the vanguard of India's future and we can safely assume that the industry shall also participate in building the infrastructure, both in private sector and in public-private partnership mode. The government, by itself, will not be able to deliver. The vestiges of License Permit Raj are yet to be wiped out completely. Even now there is bureaucratic control and political interference. It takes years for a large project that is conceived, to reach the stage of its implementation. If this bottleneck is removed, Indian industry is capable of setting up world class enterprises.

Without the basic infrastructure of roads, power, ports, airports etc. the growth would become unsustainable. For growth to become inclusive, we have to reach out to rural India and improve rural roads and connectivity, which is in a pathetic state. Banking is too distant from rural India. Almost 60 per cent of the population does not have banking facility. They have mobile phones but do not have bank accounts. RBI is contemplating granting new licenses to private parties. A condition must be imposed that for every urban branch, the new banks will open X number of branches in un-banked rural areas. A ratio will have to be worked out on a rational basis. Rural connectivity and banking will, in some measure, mitigate the poverty in spite of the bad delivery mechanism of the Government, for its welfare schemes. If rural India is provided with roads, banking and education, it will lead to an explosive growth, in the demand for goods and services which will make growth truly inclusive.

Another issue that requires urgent attention is land purchase and acquisition. There is an archaic law on land acquisition and every other day we find agitators, whose lands are being acquired by the Government, either for road or for industry. Industrialists should try to purchase land directly, by paying the market price. The Government should step in only when the land owner is blackmailing the purchaser for an exorbitant price. It may be limited to not more than 25 or 30 per cent of the land requirement cases. There is relief and rehabilitation policy but its implementation is very shabby. The rehabilitation of land-losers should be of the utmost priority for both the acquirer and the Government. Rehabilitation should not be on paper only. It should be a part of the project implementation. Employment opportunities to land-losers, should be given priority and industry should take upon itself to set up skill development centres, educational centres and see to it that the land-losers are educated and skilled to find employment.

Another area of concern is corruption, not only at the highest level but at all levels, which affects even the man on street. Successive governments have proved more corrupt than the previous ones. People have become sick of routine exposes being churned out by the media, as corruption is the staple fodder for the print and the electronic media. Laws have to be framed rationally. Merely legislating to make laws stiffer does not achieve compliance; rather people violate it and get away with and through corruption. Why open the window so wide that every one has an opportunity to find the solution, by violating the law and getting away with it? India has been active in framing such laws and rules which have very stiff provisions but there is near zero compliance. We must revisit them to find out what correction should be carried out to reduce the scope of violation and corruption.

Another sector which can lead to high growth is tourism, the hotel and aviation industies. At present, India receives only 5 million foreign tourists per year, which a single city like Singapore receives every year. Better law & order and infrastructure of airports and roads can cause huge growth in the number of foreign tourists coming into India. It will give a big boost to the services sector and bring in high investment for both aviation and hotel industries.

Now, having said all that, the fact remains that India is poised to double its economy by 2020, with the possibility of tremendous growth in industry, based on power and infrastructure. Information technology is no longer dependent on BPOs and outsourcing from US. Indian technocrats are in a position to compete with the very best in the world. The services sector will grow even higher than the industry. Service sector's growth will fuel further growth of industry. India will be consuming more than double of what it consumes today. Here, I wish to put in a word of caution that unless the issue of poverty is addressed on an urgent basis, there may be social unrest, political upheaval and internal security problems. This may erupt and jeopardise all that we are hoping to achieve.

A.B. Bardhan

Economic Growth, Development and the Working Class

On 7th September, workers, in all parts of the country, went on strike. They included men and women in organised and unorganised sectors. There were workers and employees from power mines, plantations, even small industries. Banks and insurance, government offices, both central and state; workers from coal, oil, telecom, transport, and even IT, participated in the strike. Lakhs of agricultural workers joined the strike action.

It was the biggest strike ever, and estimates put it anywhere around ten crore working people. Even Arunachal Pradesh, Meghalaya and Sikkim witnessed the strike.

It was indeed a historic strike, coming after several months of protest actions, ranging from joint conventions, mass rallies, demonstrations and jail bharo andolans, in all states and the centre. The unique feature was the inclusiveness of the strike, brought about due to the united leadership of all Central Trade Unions, ranging from the INTUC to the AITUC, CITU, HMS, AICCTU and other Left Trade Union Centres. The BMS too was a part of this united action, except on the call for the September 7 strike. However it did not oppose the strike.

What were the working people fighting against?

They were fighting against the menacing price rise of food items and all essential commodities. They were pointing an accusing finger at the yawning disparities in economic and social life. While official spokesmen were gloating over the high rate of economic growth in the country, at the ground level we were witnessing an unprecedented rise in economic inequalities. While a few had reached dizzying heights of prosperity and personal wealth, the overwhelming masses had sunk into the lowest depths of poverty and deprivation. The country presented a scene of several islands of prosperity in a vast ocean of poverty.

The struggle of the working masses against the anti-people economic policies was led by the organised working class. A section of the workers and employees had, through their organised strength and unity, improved their wages and living conditions. But they knew too well that they were a small section. The majority of their class brethren were unorganised, deprived and poor. It is their class affinity and class instinct which prompted them to head the struggle against the flawed policies.

Today when unemployment is on the rise, lakhs of vacancies are not filled up in the central and state government departments, in the railways and other PSUs. A sinister feature of unemployment is its high incidence among the educated youth.

The workers were protesting against the disinvestment of profit-making PSUs, which paves the way for their eventual privatisation. Their demand for setting up a Welfare Fund for the benefit of the unorganised labour had been responded to, only with a pitiful allocation of Rs.1000 crore. But the corporates and big business houses were rescued from the crises of their own making, by granting them financial packages and stimulus, running into lakhs of crores, not to speak of tax concessions and so forth.

Labour laws were being ignored and violated with impunity. Governments were even refusing to register trade unions, and those who tried were being dismissed from service while the Labour Department looked on, unconcerned. Every agitation by workers, was being met by severe police repression.

With the onset of the world financial and economic crises originating from America, workers had to face retrenchments, closures and job losses. There is a concerted drive to replace regular workers with contract labour.

Apart from industrial actions, the issues were raised with the Prime Minister himself, through several deputations and in personal talks by the leaders of Central Trade Unions. Mr. Sanjeeva Reddy, President INTUC, MP and a permanent invitee to the Congress Working Committee, has himself, mentioned about his talks with the Prime Minister and the Congress leadership. The matter was also raised in the Parliament on several occasions. But all pleas fell on deaf ears. The Government remained unmoved, despite several actions.

Meanwhile, the Left Parties who are closely associated with workers, peasants and other sections of urban and rural poor, had organised sustained agitations against price rise, disinvestment and the government's Neo-Liberal Economic Policies of Liberalisation, Privatisation and Globalisation.

Massive Jail Bharo Andolan, followed by a huge march to the Parliament culminating in a Bharat Bandh, had been organised.

Other opposition parties had also joined in, in the unprecedented Bharat Bandh, on the 5th of July. Thus, both at the political and trade union level working masses, the so-called 'Aam Admi' had been on the move, during the whole year. And yet the Government remained unmoved.

Can it be hoped that the Government will hearken to the loud voice raised by the multi crore toiling masses? Or, is it a futile expectation?

II

The strike on September 7 is historic, precisely because it had drawn in Central Trade Unions and their followers, belonging to different organisational affiliations and political loyalties. For the first time in 63 years, the INTUC had joined hands with the Left-led and other trade unions.

It was not a fortuitous happening, a chance event. It was a result of a long and common experience of all sections of working people about what is happening to the economy, its so-called growth, and what this has really meant for the people.

The government claims that the Indian economy is growing at a fast rate. It recorded as high as 9.4 per cent in 2006-07. For the entire period of the UPA government, the growth had averaged 7.6 per cent. The 11th Plan is projecting a growth rate of 8.5 to 9 per cent and expects that it may touch 10 per cent in the last year of the Plan. Government circles point to the soaring Sensex, to the huge foreign exchange reserves and the fact that India, today is a sought-after destination for foreign capital as signs of the confidence which foreign investors have in the Indian economy. All these are attributed to the 'economic reforms' pursued by the UPA Government.

However, during this period, the rate of unemployment has gone up from 2.78 per cent to 3.06 per cent. India's ranking in the UNDP's Human Development Index has declined from 124 in 2000 to 126 in 2004, and further down to 128 in 2006-07. Our smug officials explain this away by saying that this is not because India is doing badly but because the other countries 'have done better than India'!

The official Economic Survey claims that the current poverty level stands at 27.8 per cent. Renowned economists have challenged this figure. The official definition of poverty itself is based solely on the per-capita per day calorific need (i.e. food requirement). It does not take cognizance of any non-food needs, leave alone any saving or any possibility of investment by the poor. This approach denies the poor, any human and social aspirations of participating in the country's socio-economic processes and it is sufficient if they can buy the minimum quantity of food necessary for his survival. This is a cynical inhuman approach.

As per the Report of a government-appointed committee, the total number of people in India, belonging to the poor and vulnerable groups, having a daily per capita consumption of less than Rs. 20 in 2004-05 is 836 million, constituting about 78 per cent of our population.

About 88 per cent of India's SC/STs belong to this group of poor and vulnerable. Similarly about 85 per cent of all Muslims and 80 per cent of all OBCs, belong to this category.

There are many ways and much statistical material to reveal this shocking disparity both in India and on a world scale. The richest 20 per cent of the world's population hold almost 85 per cent of the world's wealth. The poorest 20 per cent control only 1.4 per cent. This was 2.4 per cent, only 30 years ago. In the matter of consumption, the richest one-fifth consume 86 per cent of the world output, while the poorest one-fifth consume 4 per cent of energy, 5 per cent of meat and fish etc.

For the stinking rich, this may be paradise on earth, but it is at the cost of condemning the rest of the people, to a living hell.

And yet, the government pursues policies which benefit the rich and hit the poor. This goes by the name of development.

Those who are poor are also illiterate and poorly educated. They also account for 79 per cent of the unorganised workers with informal and casual employment, with no job security, social protection or minimum wages. Poverty, unemployment, illiteracy and poor education go together.

A soaring Sensex as we see is accompanied by soaring hunger and poverty. Under the capitalist system of economic growth and the capitalist path of development, inequality is inevitable. But what we see today is a degree of ruthlessness and utter unconcern in government circles about the scale and dimension of this inequality.

In the 1990s, if the average income of the top 0.01 per cent was 150-200 times larger than the average income of the entire population, today it is several hundred times more.

Real wage is on the decline. According to the Economic Census 2005, real wages in the triennium ending 2003-04, were 11 per cent lower than in 1995-96. In sharp contrast, labour productivity tripled between 1981-2003. Wages now account for 15 per cent of the value addition in the organised sector, one of the lowest such ratios anywhere in the world. The benefits of increased labour productivity largely went to those deriving rent, interest and profit incomes rather than to the workers. Outside the organised sector, real wages for the casual workers have declined for all categories. A staggering 394.9 million workers or 86 per cent of the workforce, work in the unorganised sector, without any social security cover.

Liberalisation has led to the relaxation of labour laws and the state sponsored capitalist development has ushered in a climate of total denial of trade union rights to the workers. In the background of world recession and slow down of economy, the state-sponsored capitalism has further mounted formidable attacks on the working masses.

Eminent economist, Prof. Amit Bhaduri in his book, 'Development with Dignity' had stated: "It should be clear that there is a serious disconnection between our economic and political system." According to him, high growth does not deliver what the most poor Indians expect it to do. Further the author says, "It is a matter of shame that nearly 6 decades after Independence, we have anywhere between one-third to one-fourth of our population desperately poor, and denied the minimum conditions for human existence."

III

In a recent report titled 'Agriculture for Development', even the World Bank has refocussed on agriculture and asked that it be placed at the centre of the development agenda. It says that in the twenty-first century, agriculture continues to be a fundamental instrument for sustainable development and poverty reduction. According to the report, three out of every four poor people in developing countries, live in rural areas.

Therefore, development of agriculture is the key to the improvement of living conditions of the vast majority in the developing countries, including India. Agricultural production is important for food security, it is also the source of income for the majority of the rural population.

Since land reform has been abandoned, large land holdings still remain with landlords, kulaks, temples and maths. Of late, contract-farming, corporatisation of agricultural production has set in at a high speed, and what is left is subsistence farming, involving crores of farmers.

The farmer is being deprived of his cultivated land on which he and his family have laboured for generations, in the name of industrialisation, Special Economic Zones, big projects, for building five-star hotels, luxury resorts, and even for 18 hole golf links. Industries of course require land. But the land requisitioned and acquired is several times more than what is essential. The rest goes for real estate, for laundering black money and for earning speculative profits. All this too is a part of the development process! Meanwhile, millions of acres are lost to cultivation, which jeoparadises the country's food sovereignty. Several millions of families, who depend on agriculture, are uprooted and displaced, without any hope of proper rehabilitation and decent livelihood in the future. The colonial era Land Acquisition Act, 1894 continues to be used for the purpose. There is a never-ending wait for its replacement by a more farmer-friendly, just and rational law. Even land ceiling laws, which limit the land in possession of individual farmers, are being amended and relaxed, for the needs of non-agricultural purposes.

Irrigation, the key to increased agricultural production, has been shamefully overlooked. Nearly one-third of the cultivable land that is irrigated, produces more than half of the total agricultural output, while the remaining two-thirds, i.e. nearly 95 million hectares, produces the rest.

With food production dropping below the population growth rate, there has been a reduction in the per capita availability of food. As such, India has lost its food sovereignty; it has to import food, even at a higher price, than the ruling domestic market price.

A Commission constituted by the Ministry of Labour, Government of India, finally confirmed that the gains of the economic growth has not touched the overwhelming majority of the population, and as such the process of development is far from being inclusive.

Due to wrong policies, huge indebtedness has overtaken the entire farming community. The NSS 59th Round reiterates that indebtedness has increased from 26 per cent in 1991, to 48 per cent in 2003. One recalls with horror, that in the previous decade, nearly two lakh farmers committed suicide due to indebtedness. Loan-Waiver is a one-time relief measure, not a solution of the problem of chronic indebtedness.

One should therefore distinguish between economic growth per se and development. The harsh reality is that high economic growth and social development are moving divergently.

IV

The much-hyped fast economic growth has not solved or even mitigated the basic problems of poverty, unemployment, and hunger of vast masses. Rather it has aggravated them. As the economy grew, the lion's share flowed into the coffers of the small section at the top, leaving the rest high and dry. Actually it has been a bonanza for the corporate sector and big business houses, along with benefits to a top layer of the middle class. The increasing exploitation of labour is shown by the fact that while during this period of corporate-led growth, profits surged by over 13 times, the wage bill rose by only 2.24 times. An ILO report shows that between 1990 and 2002, labour productivity went up by 84 per cent, but real wages in the manufacturing sector declined by 22 per cent.

Ever since high economic growth is being tom-tomed about, unemployment has been on the rise, regional disparities are widening and inequalities of income, wealth and consumption are fast increasing. A virulent fever of vulgar and competitive display of wealth in living style, marriages, anniversaries, religious and social celebrations has gripped the affluent sections. The malady of conspicuous and pointless consumerism is spreading among this section. And those lower down are trying to ape them. This is tearing the fabric of social harmony and breeding social tensions. The fever of consumerism is blinding many people to the social reality of the dangers of globalisation.

Globalisation is the term under which imperialism presents itself today. James Petras, Professor Emeritus of Sociology at the State University of New York, and Prof. Henry Veltmeyer of Mexico have concluded, as follows, in their book "Globalisation Unmasked":

"To the extent that Globalisation rhetoric persists, it has become an ideological mask disguising the emerging power of US Corporations to exploit and enrich themselves to an unprecedented degree. Globalisation can be seen as a code word for the ascendancy of US imperialism".

Indian ruling circles, whether it was the BJP led NDA or today the Congress led UPA, not only consider this US corporate driven globalisation to be inevitable and irresistible, but are actually collaborating and succumbing to it. They consider this to be the only way to ride to the high table of the G-8 powers (which is quite unnecessary, since no issue can be settled today without taking India, China, Brazil and South Africa on board). That is why they are resorting to several collaboration agreements with the US in the spheres of defence, economy and education. As a consequence, there is a pronounced pro-US tilt in foreign policy and in international spheres as well.

The relentless pursuit of neoliberal 'economic reforms' has brought up strata of powerful corporate houses within the bourgeois class. Helped by government policies of pampering this section, the corporate houses have accumulated unprecedented wealth and thereby wield tremendous economic power. They are private monopolies in several vital sectors, such as oil, power, telecommunication and pose serious challenge to the public sector in these sphere. They are even attempting, with government help, to penetrate and take over a number of public sector undertakings, which compete with them. In their ruthless quest for super profits, they are spreading their tentacles to other spheres of economy, and also extend operations abroad, through mergers and acquisitions. They are both collaborating and competing with multinational corporations, helping them to set up bases in India. With their economic and financial clout, they are able, not only to influence but also lay down government policies in certain spheres.

Powerful sections of the media (with some honourable exceptions) have been virtually taken over by them. 'Paid News' is a small part of the bourgeois control over the media. In fact, there is growing intertwining of the corporate entities and the media moghuls, which is subverting the freedom of the press.

With Mammon installed as God, conditions have been created for large-scale corruption and the play of money power in national life. Democracy and democratic path of development are being seriously threatened. The latest dimensions of corruption in high places run into five and sometime six digits. Corruption, gross disparities and inequalities have made the entire development process one of excluding overwhelming masses from it. The exposure and fight against corruption is an integral part of the struggle for real inclusive development.

It has become more than evident that capitalism cannot solve the problems of poverty, hunger, illiteracy and disease. The myth of the omnipotence of the neo-liberal system, with America at the helm, has truly exploded. The financial crisis and the economic meltdown, which has proved worse than the Great Depression of the 1930s, has brought misery to millions of workers and other sections of the people.

It had disastrous effect on the economy of all countries of the world. Bourgeois governments have tried everywhere to shift the burden of the crisis on to the shoulders of the common people. If the impact of the crisis was not severe in India, it is thanks to the Left and the Trade Union movement which pulled the brake and prevented the government from moving ahead with its drastic liberlisation programme. Yet the Government has learnt no lesson and persists on the same path.

What the country needs is an alternative programme, a pro-people and inclusive development strategy. Such a strategy has to be based on land reforms which defend interests of farmers and agricultural labourers, an employment-friendly policy of economic growth. It has to be a policy which protects the environment and prevents the unrestrained loot and plunder of the earth's natural resources. Such a policy should stand up for the farmers' right to land, the youth's right to education and work, the people's right to food, shelter and healthcare, the tribal's right to his habitat and access to the resources of this earth. Only such strategy can expand and develop the domestic market for the products of the country's industry and agriculture and help attain a more equitable world trade regime. Only such a policy will improve the living conditions of all sections of the people and make economic growth inclusive. This requires that the present class rule be replaced by a different class combination. The growing and broadening militant struggle, that draws in ever newer sections of the toiling masses for Food, Jobs, Land, Shelter, Economic and Social Equality, for an Inclusive Development Strategy, can bring about this transformation.

S. Ayyappan & Ramesh Chand

Indian Agriculture: An Economic Perspective

Agriculture is the core sector of Indian economy. The share of agriculture and allied sectors in total GDP presently is about 16 per cent and it engages nearly 52 per cent of the national workforce. Agriculture therefore continues to remain the principal source of livelihood for the majority of households in India. Agriculture sector also sustains food security of a large percentage of population of this country which has increased from 361 million to 1180 million between 1951 and 2010. Technological progress, enabling policy framework and adequate investments, have proved to be the key drivers of agricultural growth.

Broad Characteristics of Indian Agriculture

Agriculture in India is the main occupation of millions of peasants who follow mixed crop and livestock farming. The bulk of farming units comprise of small land holdings with a preponderance of owner cultivation. The number of operational holdings has been increasing at a fast rate due to the population pressure and also due to the lack of adequate employment opportunities, outside the agriculture sector. During the three decades between 1960-61 and 1990-91, the net area available for cultivation increased by only 7.5 per cent but the number of holdings during the same period, increased by about 21.8 per cent. Because of this, the average size of land holding declined from 2.69 hectares during 1960-61 to 1.55 hectares during 1990-91. During the next decade, the net sown area in the country showed a small decline, whereas the number of land holdings increased by 13 per cent to reach a level of 120.822 million. Consequently, the proportion of marginal holdings of the size, below 1 hectare, reached 63 per cent of the total holdings during 200-01 while 82 per cent holdings were below 2 hectare (Table 1).

Table 1: Major characteristics of Indian Agriculture Unit: Million hectares

Particulars	1950/ 51	1970/ 71	1990/ 91	2000/ 01
1. Geographic area	328.7	328.7	328.7	328.7
2. Reporting area	284.3	303.8	304.9	306.2
3. Net sown area	118.8	140.3	143.0	141.1
	41.8	46.2	46.9	46.1
4. Number of holdings: million	--	70.49	106.6	120.8
5. Average farm size (ha.)	--	2.30	1.55	1.32
6. Net irrigated area	20.8	31.1	48.02	55.08
	(17.5)	(22.2)	(33.6)	(39.0)
7. Area sown more than once	13.1	25.5	42.7	46.8
	(11.0)	(18.2)	(29.9)	(33.2)

Note: Figures in italics are per cent of reporting area and figures in parentheses are per cent of net sown area.
Source: Agricultural Statistics at a Glance, various issues, Ministry of Agriculture, GOI, New Delhi.

The second important characteristic of Indian agriculture is that despite tremendous expansion in major, medium and minor irrigation, only about 40 per cent of the cultivated area has access to irrigation and the rest remains dependent on rainfall. The third important feature of Indian agriculture is that only one crop is cultivated on most of the area. More than one crop is raised only on a third of the cultivated area. The fourth feature of India's agriculture is that it is excessively crowded due to the population pressure. The availability of cultivated land per worker remains low, which has actually declined from 1.22 hectares during 1950-51 to 0.77 hectare in 1990-91 and to 0.60 hectare during 2000-01. The development policies and technology therefore for this sector must be customised to the characteristics and needs of small-holder agriculture that is largely rainfed.

Production Profile of Agriculture

India is a vast country with diverse agro-ecologies that are conducive to produce a wide range of food and non-food agri-commodities. Indian farmers have adjusted production profiles in line with the emerging opportunities, which can be seen from the changes in the composition of output of this sector between crops and livestock and share of different crops/crop groups in the value of crop output (Table 2).

Table 2: Changing profile of agriculture production in India in value terms

Group/commodity	1970-71	1980-81	1990-91	2000-01	2007-08
Share in total agriculture output %					
Crop sector	85.14	82.65	76.93	73.30	73.10
Livestock sector	14.86	17.35	23.07	26.70	26.90
Share in crop output%					
Cereals	43.90	37.86	34.92	31.94	29.94
Rice	24.08	19.39	18.86	16.81	14.54
Wheat	10.06	10.53	10.71	11.09	10.95
Pulses	5.30	6.34	6.69	4.41	4.71
Chickpea	2.12	2.64	2.44	1.60	1.72
Oilseeds	9.88	8.70	13.27	7.02	10.58
Groundnut	4.92	3.29	4.77	2.17	3.46
Sugarcane	5.51	8.00	6.73	6.88	5.15
Cotton	3.68	3.28	3.35	2.47	4.88
Fruit & vegetables	15.55	16.89	18.04	25.58	25.77

Source: National Accounts Statistics, Central Statistical Organisation, Government of India, New Delhi, various issues.

An analysis of the composition of agricultural output shows increase in the share of livestock output over the years. Livestock constituted less than 15 per cent of the total agriculture output in 1970-71 and in the next three and a half decades, its share increased to about 27 per cent. Significant changes have also been experienced in the composition of crop output. Cereals continue to dominate crop output though their share has followed a sharp decline from close to 44 per cent during 1970-71 to 30 per cent during 2007-08. The share of fruits and vegetables in the total value of crops increased from 15.55 per cent to 25.77 per cent in the same period.

Paddy/rice is the most important crop of the country, which alone accounts for more than 20 per cent of the value of all crops produced in the country. Wheat is the second most important crop produced in India. Its share in the total crop output has remained stable around 10.5 per cent. The productivity and production of rice and wheat have shown constant increases even though the area under respective crops is nearly stable since the last 3-4 decades. (Tables 3 and 3a).

Table 3 : Area, productivity and production of Rice in India

Year	Area -mha	Yield-kg/ha	Production-mt
1965-66	35.47	862	30.59
1970-71	37.59	1123	42.22
1980-81	40.15	1336	53.63
1990-91	42.69	1740	74.29
1999-2000	45.16	1986	89.68
2008-09	45.35	2186	99.15

Table 3a : Area, productivity and production of Wheat in India

Year	Area -mha	Yield-kg/ha	Production-mt
1965-66	12.57	827	10.40
1970-71	18.24	1307	23.83
1980-81	22.28	1630	36.31
1990-91	24.17	2281	55.14
1999-2000	27.49	2778	76.37
2008-09	27.88	2891	80.58

Source: Agricultural Statistics at a glance-2009, Directorate of Economics and Statistics, DAC, MOA, GOI

Production of pulses in India has recorded low growth over the years. Due to the supply constraints, prices of pulses have been rising at a faster rate, compared to those of other crops. This resulted in the increase in the share of pulses and in the value of crop output, during 1970-71 and 1990-91. Chickpea is the most important pulse crop of the country but its share, like other pulses, witnessed decline after 1990-91.

The share of oilseeds showed an increase from 8.7 per cent in 1980-81 to 13.27 per cent in 1990-91 as this decade experienced almost doubling of the oilseeds production in the country. This could happen due to the several measures undertaken by the government to make India self-sufficient in oilseeds during the mid-and-late 1980s. These include measures like Technology Mission on Oilseeds and National Oilseeds Development Project.

Among individual crops, sugarcane occupies the third position in terms of output contribution in value terms, after rice and wheat. Cotton is another important cash crop of India, which contributes more than three per cent of the total crop output. Its contribution suffered serious setback around 2000-01 but with the infusion of new technologies, it has recovered the lost ground in the recent years. The share of fruits and vegetables, which comprise of a very large amount of produce, has shown improvement throughout. Highest gains were recorded during 1990-91 to 2000-01, with the contribution of fruits and vegetables to crop output witnessing an increase from 18.04 per cent to 25.58 per cent.

Status of Agriculture in Indian Economy

Agriculture is considered the backbone of Indian economy and the growth rate of the economy is strongly influenced by the performance of agriculture. The reason underlying this assertion is that among the nine major sectors, agriculture remains the largest sector of the economy. Its contribution to total GDP during 1950-51 was more than 55 per cent. Over time, as it happens in a developing economy, the share of agriculture in the national output, started declining. Between 1980-81 and 2000-01, the share of agriculture in national income declined from 35.7 per cent to 23.3 per cent. However, the workforce engaged in agriculture in the same period, witnessed a very small decline, from 60.5 per cent to 58.4 per cent. This is in contrast to the experience of the developed countries, where the share of agriculture in employment, declined much more sharply, with the decline in agriculture's share in GDP.

Table 4: Share of Agriculture in Output and Employment in Indian Economy

Year	Share of agriculture in GDP	Share of agriculture in Employment
1980-81	35.7	60.5
1990-91	29.2	59.0
2000-01	23.3	58.4
2008-09	15.7	52.1@

Note: Agriculture includes crops, livestock, fishery and forestry.
@: Based on Current daily status for year 2004-05.

During the last one decade, some adverse trends have emerged in Indian agriculture. The per capita income for the population, dependent on agriculture, is not growing. Disparities between per worker income in agriculture and non-agriculture are widening. Inter-regional variations in agriculture productivity are high and have been rising. Moreover, the natural resource base of agriculture is shrinking and there are signs of degradation of land and overexploitation of water in the country. Food security of the country, achieved through hard labour of the last four decades, is also seen to be under threat.

Agriculture Growth and Farm Income

The series on growth rate indicate that different phases of growth coincide with different phases of agricultural policy. In the pre Green Revolution period, net area under cultivation increased from 118 million hectare to 138 million hectare. Despite large expansion in area, GDP agriculture experienced 2.66 per cent average annual growth rate. Adoption of high yielding varieties during late 1960s led to substantial increase in productivity of two principal crops grown in India, wheat and paddy, which raised output growth to 2.76 per cent during 15 years, following onset of the Green Revolution. Initially, adoption of Green Revolution technology remained concentrated in north west plains and some areas in southern India, both of which had assured water supply for irrigation. Around 1980-81, improved technology spread to several other regions and agricultural economy diversified. This resulted in further acceleration in growth of agricultural output. Output growth improved considerably around late 1960s. In 1979-80, India faced very severe drought which caused a dip in agricultural output. After that, agricultural output followed accelerated growth trend till 1995-96, after which agricultural output again moved on a lower growth trajectory.

The series on growth rate indicate that different phases of growth coincide with different phases of agricultural policy and technology. In the pre Green Revolution period, the net area under cultivation increased from 118 million hectare to 138 million hectare. Despite the large expansion in area, agriculture experienced 2.66 per cent average annual growth rate.

Table 5: Growth rate in GDP agriculture and non agriculture sectors in different periods, at 1993-94 prices: per cent/year

Period	Total economy	Non-agriculture	Agriculture
I. Pre green revolution 1950/51 to 1964/65	3.95	5.59	2.66
II Green revolution period 1965/66 to 1979/80	3.62	4.40	2.76
III Wider technology dissemination period 1980/81 to 1994/95	5.37	6.56	3.33
IV Post reforms 1995/96 to 2007/08	6.61	7.80	2.64

The adoption of high yielding variety seeds, during the late 1960s, led to substantial increase in productivity of the two principal crops, namely wheat and paddy, which raised output growth to 2.76 per cent during the first fifteen years, following the onset of the Green Revolution.

Around 1980-81, the improved agricultural technologies spread to several other regions, leading to diversification of agricultural economy.

This resulted in the further acceleration of the growth of agricultural output. This period also witnessed sharp acceleration in the growth rate of the non- agriculture sector. After mid-1990s, however, the growth rate of agricultural output declined sharply.

This slowdown caused a severe impact on the income of those who are dependent on agriculture. This is evident in the level and growth in per worker farm income during the 5 years, centred on 1971, 1981, 1991 and 2001 for which census estimates are available. Per worker farm income increased annually by 1.08 per cent during the 1970s. The growth rate accelerated to 1.16 per cent during 1980s. However, during the last decade per worker farm income increased merely by 0.28 per cent.

Table 6: Level and growth in per worker farm income at 1993-94 prices

Period	Agricultural income per worker Rs.	Growth rate in income in previous 10 years % / year
1968/ 9 to 1973/ 4	8947	
1978/ 9 to 1983/ 4	9961	1.08
1988/ 9 to 1993/ 4	11179	1.16
1998/ 9 to 2003/ 4	11496	0.28

Source: Chand (2008).

Rural Urban Disparity

Large gap in the performance of agriculture and non-agriculture sectors has created wide disparities between rural and urban India. Faster growth in the output of non-agriculture sector did not help much in shifting workforce from agriculture to non-agriculture sector. Between 1980-81 and 2000-01, the share of agriculture in national income declined from 38.8 per cent to 25.5 per cent. But the workforce engaged in agriculture in the same period witnessed a very small decline, from 60.5 per cent to 52.5 per cent (Table 4). Slow growth in agriculture, with no significant decline in labour force, has created a serious disparity between agriculture and non-agriculture and urban and rural India. The magnitude of this can be seen from per worker income in agriculture and non-agriculture sectors presented in Table 6. During the two decades after 1980/81, per worker income in non-agriculture sector has more than doubled whereas in agriculture this increase is less than 12 per cent. As a consequence, one worker in non-agriculture sector earns more than the income of five workers in agriculture. This disparity is causing a lot of concerns in the country.

Table 7: Per worker income in agriculture and non agriculture sectors at 1993/94 prices

Period	Income per worker Rs.		Ratio of non agri
	Agri	Non agri	to agri income
1978/ 9 to 1983/ 4	9961	28430	2.85
1988/ 9 to 1993/ 4	11179	39355	3.52
1998/ 9 to 2003/ 4	11496	59961	5.22

Source: Chand (2008).

Inter Regional Disparities

Some regions of the country are agriculturally well-developed and have successfully experienced socio-economic transformation through improvement in agricultural productivity and the consequent growth. The extent of regional variations in the agricultural sector can be seen from Fig.1. Further, regional variations in NSDP (Net State Domestic Product) per ha cultivated area, increased from 54 per cent during 1984 to 1986 to 66 per cent, during 2003 to 2005.

Sustainability

India has only 4 per cent of the world's total water resources and over 17 per cent share in population. Obviously, the water scarcity is more acute in the country, compared to the world average. Demand for water is rising rapidly for non-agricultural uses as well as agricultural uses. The more serious conflict is seen in the case of use of water in agriculture. In the case of groundwater, this conflict is reflected in present v/s future use of

Fig. 1: Inter state variations in productivity of crop sector during three years ending with 2005-6.

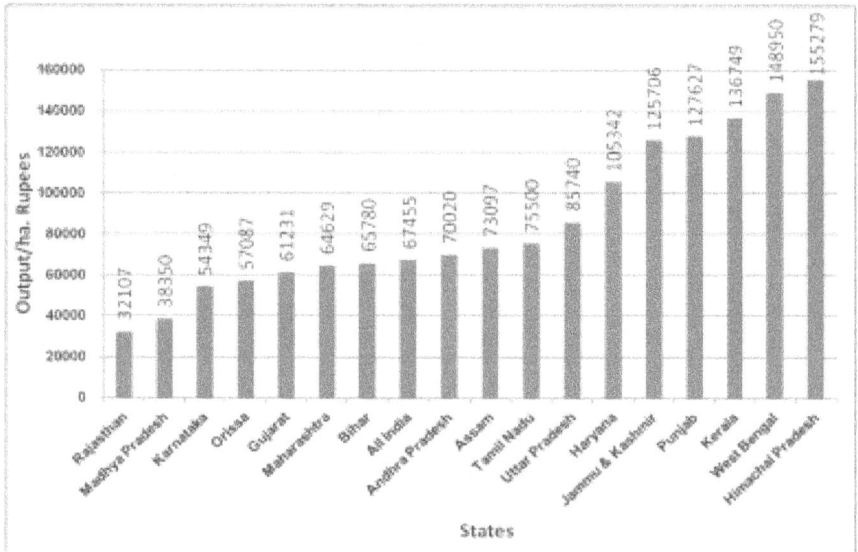

water and in the case of surface water (river water) the conflict is seen in inter-state water disputes, over sharing of river water. These kinds of incidences are expected to increase in future.

According to some scholars, the availability of ground water for irrigation would emerge as a critical bottleneck for self-sufficiency in foodgrain by the year 2020, as demand for irrigation would exceed its availability by nearly 30 per cent (Chopra and Goldar 2000). Similarly, National Commission for Integrated Water Resource Development Plan has projected that the requirement for irrigation water in India would grow by more than 50 per cent by 2050. Based on various assessments, it is concluded that even after fully exploiting available water resources, water supply can match the demand only if there is a big improvement in the efficiency of irrigation.

Water table in several states is depleting at an alarming rate. In some parts, like north-west India, it is leading to lowering of water table, and in some parts, in the hard rock areas of the peninsular India, overexploitation of water has led to mining of water from deeper and deeper aquifers and ultimately, to borewell failure. Even in the Indo-Gangetic region, which is known to have adequate water resources for providing assured irrigation and where shallow tubewells have brought about Green Revolution, farmers have started digging borewells deeper and deeper because groundwater in upper aquifers, have depleted.

While demand for water is rising rapidly, the water resource in rivers is also declining. This is happening because of siltation in rivers and degradation of watersheds, due to deforestation and increased human activities.

Food Security

India achieved impressive growth in foodgrain production after the adoption of Green Revolution technology. Per capita production of foodgrains increased from 183 kg during the early 1970s to 207 kg by mid-1990s, despite the increase in population by more than 50 per cent. However, after the mid-1990s, foodgrain production did not keep pace with population growth. Per capita production of cereals has declined by 17 kg and the production of pulses by 2 kg, during the last decade (Table 8).

Table 8: Per capita production of foodgrains, Kg: 1971 to 2009

Year	Cereals	Pulses	Foodgrains
1971-75	164	19	183
1976-80	172	18	190
1981-85	179	17	196
1986-90	182	16	198
1991-95	192	15	207
1996-00	191	14	205
2001-05	177	12	189
2006-09	174	13	184

Source: Economic Survey, GoI, New Delhi, Various issues.

In contrast to foodgrains, production of all other food items like fruits, vegetables, milk, eggs, meat, fish and sugar has remained much higher than the population growth which has resulted in considerable improvement in per capita production and per capita consumption of livestock, horticultural and fishery products.

It is interesting to point out that the decline in per capita production of cereals has coincided with a sharp increase in the export of cereals from the country. This underscores the need for improving purchasing power of the low-income consumers along with an increase in the production of cereals and pulses, to keep pace with the growth in population of the country.

The Future

Given the vital importance of agriculture for food security and livelihood of the majority of the population as well as for the overall growth of the economy, the country needs an effective strategy to address the problems and challenges that confront Indian agriculture. There is also a need for policies and strategies to adjust to new ecologies, changing demand patterns, upcoming value chains and supermarkets, revolution in communication technology, institutional innovations and globalisation as well as other evolving changes in the system surrounding agriculture. Elimination of poverty, improvement in nutrition and supply of safe food are of prime importance for every country. It is important to emphasise that no production activity can be sustained in the long run by overlooking the health of the production base and the producers. In this context, it is essential that we focus on farmers and the natural resource system comprising land, water, vegetation etc. which forms the production base of agriculture. Often, policies are focussed on farming without taking into account their implications for the farmers. Unless growth and development of farming leads to improvement in the welfare of farmers, it cannot be sustained.

Diversification of agriculture towards high value agricultural commodities like fruits, vegetables and dairy products holds vast potential to accelerate growth and improve farm income in the country. Harnessing full benefits of such diversification, requires new institutional and contractual arrangements for production and marketing and ensuring that smallholders are not excluded from the process.

Accelerating Growth in Output and Farm Income

Growth in agricultural output and farm income depends upon a large number of factors viz. prices of output and inputs, technology and other non-price factors. Raising agricultural growth requires remunerative pricing of environment for output, access to improved technology, application of quality inputs and machinery. Moreover, growth has to be achieved from a shrinking natural resource base which implies that growth comes primarily from the increase in productivity.

Terms of trade for agriculture during 1997 to 2005 remained adverse and are identified as one of the factors for poor performance of agriculture during this period. Due to the increased use of agricultural produce for bio fuel and feed as well as several other constraints on the supply side, prices of agricultural products are expected to shift to a higher equilibrium. Projections are that prices of farm produce would remain high in short to medium term, which would offer remunerative price environment, provided these higher prices are transmitted to farm level.

An exercise done for the Eleventh Plan shows that in order to achieve 4 per cent growth rate in agriculture, India would need to raise public investment in real terms by 12 per cent and private investment by 3.5 per cent. Area under fruits and vegetables and use of fertilizer should increase at the rate of 2.5 per cent each. However, growth in these factors alone would not translate into 4 per cent growth in output, therefore action would be needed in several other areas also.

Technology

Technology is the prime mover for growth. Considering the costs and constraints of resources such as water, nutrients and energy, the genetic enhancement of productivity should be coupled with input use efficiency. This can be made possible only by creation and utilisation of new and improved technology.

Agriculture research system has demonstrated, at farmers' field, a large number of promising technologies to achieve high growth and promote farming systems that improve natural resource base. However, these are not seen at farmers' fields at large. Frontline demonstrations of various departments provide clinching evidences of large gaps between what can be attained at farmers' fields with the adoption of improved technology and what is obtained with the existing practices followed by the farmers. This is a clear pointer to the large potential for raising output through the effective dissemination of technology, especially in the eastern Gangetic Plains. But this is not happening because of the absence or weak Research-Extension-Farmer linkages. The reason is marketing of technology. As public extension systems are proving increasingly inadequate for dissemination of technology, there is a need to involve the private sector in marketing and dissemination of technology. This requires increased public-private sector participation through appropriate returns and incentives for the innovators and disseminators.

Seed and other Inputs

Good quality seed is the primary determinant of productivity. Often, farmers do not distinguish between grain and seed, and the seed replacement rate is very low. The main reason for this is non-availability of quality seeds and to some extent, awareness. Harnessing benefits of technology generation requires a well developed system for sales and distribution of seeds and plant propagation material. Up until now, public sector has dominated multiplication and supply of seeds and plant propagation materials but it is highly inadequate to meet the emerging and growing needs and demand. The unscrupulous private trade is taking undue advantage of this inadequacy. There is an urgent need to develop competitive seed industry by involving private sector in seed production and distribution.

The existing production firms are not able to cater to the rising demand for fertilizers, agro-chemicals and other inputs. The problem of shortage is exploited by supply of spurious seeds and pesticides. India needs to attract more investments in these areas.

Sustainable Use of Natural Resources

Land and water need special attention for their sustainable use. Large tracts of land in East India (acidic soils) and other places in the country need special treatments and reclamations which would enhance their productivity. Resource conserving technologies are now available for various ecological regions. These can be very helpful to save water and energy, reduce cost and increase farmers' income. Adequate emphasis and investments are needed to harvest and conserve rain water and optimally use available water.

About two third of our arable land remain without use for most part of the year. Increase in cropping intensity by various means is an effective way to cope with land constraint.

Since water is emerging as the main constraining factor, particular attention needs to be given to check wastage. Land and water need to be used efficiently and on a sustainable basis. Rain water going waste needs to be tapped and conserved. Major emphasis is needed on water conservation and recharging schemes, including restoration and renovation of traditional water bodies, as an integral part of watershed development, with the involvement of local communities and NGOs. There is need for a paradigm shift in promoting agricultural productivity, not only per unit of area but also per unit of water and time.

Pricing policy on inputs like water and fertilizer should be such to promote sustainable use of land and water and balanced use of fertilizer. Attention to soil healthcare needs to be given high priority. Soil health cards, giving regularly updated information on major and micronutrients, should be issued to all the farmers. This would require strengthening of soil testing labs in all parts of the country. Provision of micronutrients like zinc, boron and sulphur can help to increase crop yield by over 50 per cent, especially in dry land farming areas. At the same time, production and sale of bio-fertilizers, e.g. compost, organic manure and micronutrients, should be encouraged on a large scale, through informal as well as organised production systems, by providing appropriate incentives.

Farm Structure

Farm size in India is quite small. More than 61 per cent holdings are below 1 hectare and more than 80 per cent are below 2 hectares. Furthermore, 60 per cent of the cultivated areas being non-irrigated, the options to go for high value agriculture, at such farms, are highly limited. These farms face serious constraints in adopting modern technology and in marketing their produce. To some extent, size disadvantage can be obviated through contract farming. In most cases, the size of farm would remain unviable and insufficient to provide enough income for the farmers and their families. There are two ways to raise size of operational holdings. One, to create suitable jobs in the non-agriculture sector to attract or pull out unviable marginal and small farmers from agriculture sector. Two, to liberalise land lease markets so that those who want to rent out land can do that without fear of losing ownership rights.

Biotechnology

Some countries have very effectively applied tools of biotechnology to raise yield, reduce cost of production, and improve quality of some edible oilseeds, which has imparted them significant advantage. There are also reports of large areas being brought under transgenic crops namely soybean, cotton and vegetables in countries like USA, Argentina, Canada and China. The new biotech crops can help in developing drought tolerance, and reduce use of inputs and water. These could be effectively deployed for enhancing crop productivity.

Marketing and Trade Policies

Assured marketing and prices provide the best incentives for farmers to invest in agriculture. Crops like pulses, oilseeds, maize, pearl millet and soybean etc. need market support as do wheat and rice. In the case of a number of crops in many markets, the actual price remained lower than MSP and in some cases the gap is very large. This is because there are no arrangements for procurement at support prices for quite a few crops in several parts of the country. The farmers feel that they do not get genuine price for their produce while consumers feel that they are being charged higher price without much value addition on farm produce. This can be addressed by reducing marketing margins and wastages and by improving efficiency of production and marketing. Private sector should be encouraged to forge efficient linkages between production and consumption by setting up value chains, contract farming, processing, direct marketing, etc. to benefit producers as well consumers.

Distress sale crops/commodities below MSP is now not uncommon. Agriculture growth in such conditions/situations is stifled due to weak or missing institutional support in the form of guaranteed price. Extension of government intervention in foodgrain markets, like implementing MSP and procurement, would help in exploiting agricultural potential and help to sustain food security of the country.

India's economic security will continue to be predicated upon the Agriculture sector, in the foreseeable future. The research approach will have to rely on the development and application of cutting-edge science, improving quality of inputs and their use efficiency, supported by state-of-the-art infrastructure, an enlightened human resource, active involvement of all stakeholders while maintaining and building on the health of the primary production base, etc. The National Agricultural Research System under the aegis of the ICAR, has, in the past, served a very useful purpose and improved the national food security and in this endeavour, will continue to strive to achieve a sustainable national food and nutritional security and prosperity through excellence in agricultural research and education.

References

Chand, Ramesh (2008), 'The State of Indian Agriculture and Prospects for the Future', in Chopra, Kanchan and Rao, C.H. Hanumantha (Eds.) "Growth Equity, Environment and Population", Sage Publications India, New Delhi.

Chopra, Kanchan and Goldar, Bishwanath (2000), "Sustainable Development Framework for India: The Case of Water Resources", Institute of Economic Growth, Delhi.

Planning Commission (2007), "Report of the Steering Committee on Agriculture for the Eleventh Five Year Plan (2007-2012)", Government of India, New Delhi.

C.P. Chandrasekhar

International Finance and India

Among the features quoted to establish India's post-liberalisation economic success, is the special relationship it has developed with international finance. Not only has India become a much-favoured destination for international investors, especially financial investors, but India's foreign exchange reserves have, for some time now, been extremely comfortable. India's foreign exchange reserves rose by a huge $110.5 billion during the financial year 2007-08 to touch $309.7 billion as on March 31, 2008. This increase occurred primarily because of the huge inflow of foreign capital. Viewed in terms of the need to finance current transactions, which had, in the past, influenced policies regarding foreign exchange use and allocation, India is now foreign exchange rich in that despite the global financial crisis, even in August 2010, India had a $280 billion plus foreign exchange reserve, which exceeded the value of 10 months' imports. The country has clearly come a long way from the situation in 1991, when it faced a balance of payments crisis with reserves having fallen to levels equal to the value of two weeks' imports. This transition from paucity to surplus has led to the view that foreign capital inflows are intrinsically good for the country, since they not only shore up the balance of payments, but also help finance investments, especially in core areas, like infrastructure.

When views of this kind are expressed, what is often forgotten is that India's success as a global player is not because of a current account surplus resulting from its export performance; rather, it stems from the inflows of capital that far exceeds its current account financing requirements. This implies that our foreign exchange reserves are a reflection, not of our export success, which was what liberalisation was expected to deliver, but has accumulated because of large foreign capital inflow. In sum, our reserves are not earned (as is true of China with its current account surpluses), but borrowed.

The celebration of this status that the country has acquired, points to a dramatic shift in the government's perceptions of the role of foreign finance in the country's development. In the 1950s, the view was that consolidating political freedom required winning freedom from foreign capital. Controls on foreign capital were therefore seen as needed for creating the domestic policy space to implement strategies that would deliver growth and bring about self-reliance. It was also believed that excessive reliance on Foreign Direct Investment would result in the drain of surpluses which would subvert growth - a successful growth strategy must therefore deliver results without excessive foreign exchange expenditure.

Given this background, India's transition to a liberal and open economic policy regime is an event of great historical significance. The question as to why and how this transition occurred, the effect it had on the pace and pattern of the growth of the economy and its outcomes in the form of employment generation and distribution are still being debated. What is clear is that the transition did not occur because of the loss of momentum under the post-Independence import-substitution strategy. That loss of momentum had occurred much earlier and was caused by the crisis of the mid-1960s, following which our economy experienced a period of secular stagnation, till the 1980s.

Three mutually reinforcing and interrelated contradictions in the post-Independence growth strategy were the reasons behind the stagnation. To start with, despite the talk of land reform, of providing "land-to-the-tiller" and curbing the concentration of economic power, little was done to attack and redress prevalent assets and income. One consequence of the resulting persistence of asset and income inequality, was that there were definite limits to the expansion of the market for mass consumption goods in the country. The large mass of peasantry, faced with insecure conditions of tenure and often obtaining a small share in the outputs they produced, had neither the means nor the incentive to invest. The prospect of increasing productivity and incomes in rural India, which continues to be home to the majority of its population, in order to stimulate domestic demand, was therefore limited. The absence of any radical land redistribution had meant that the domestic market, especially for the industrial goods, had remained narrowly-based.

Under these circumstances, a continuous growth in State spending was essential for the growth of the market. Therefore, the stimulus to growth during the early post-independence years came from the State itself. It provided domestic capitalists with a large market by widening and intensifying protection and displacing imported goods from the domestic market. It sought to expand the market through its current and capital expenditures and supported the domestic capitalist class by investing in crucial infrastructural sectors and channelising household savings to finance private investment, through the creation of a number of industrial development banks.

This strategy did pay dividends during the decade-and-a-half immediately following Independence when rates of industrial growth were creditable by the international standards. By the mid-1960s, however, not only did the stimulus offered by the import substitution strategy get exhausted, the ability of the State to continue to provide the stimulus to growth, was also undermined. As a consequence, growth decelerated, leading to the "secular stagnation" in the late-1960s and 1970s. This is the second of the contradictions that characterised the process of development. The State within the old economic policy regime had to simultaneously fulfil two different roles that proved incompatible in the long-run. On the one hand it had to maintain growing expenditures, in particular investment expenditure, in order to keep the domestic market expanding. At the same time however the State exchequer was the medium through which large-scale transfers were made to the capitalist and proto-capitalist groups; the State, in other words, was an instrument for the "primary accumulation of capital". The contradiction between these two different roles of the State manifested itself in the deepening of fiscal crisis. The implications of this growing fiscal crisis were obvious: the government would sooner or later have to cut down its expenditure, especially investment expenditure, which would slow down the economy and eventually arouse capitalists' demands for an alternative policy regime.

The final contradiction had its roots in the cultural ambience of an ex-colonial society like India. The market for the industrial goods was, from its very inception, as we have seen, a socially narrowly-based one. Capitalism in its metropolitan centres however is characterised by continuous product innovation, the phenomenon of newer and ever newer goods being thrown on to the market, resulting in alterations of life-styles. In an ex-colonial economy like India, the comparatively narrow social segment to whose hands additional purchasing power accrues in a large measure and whose growing consumption therefore provides the main source of the growth in demand for industrial consumer goods, is also anxious to emulate the life-styles prevailing in the metropolitan centres. It is not satisfied with having more and more of the same goods which are domestically produced, nor is it content merely with expending its additional purchasing power upon such new goods, as the domestic economy, on its own, is capable of innovating. Its demand is for the new goods which are being produced and consumed in the metropolitan centres, and which, given the constraints upon the innovative capacity of the domestic economy, are incapable of being locally produced, purely on the basis of indigenous resources and indigenous technology.

An imbalance therefore inevitably arises in such economies between what the economy is capable of locally producing purely on its own steam and what the relatively affluent sections of society, who account for much of the growth of potential demand for consumer goods, would like to consume. This imbalance may be kept in check by import controls, though such controls inevitably give rise to clandestine imports, through smuggling, which are sold in local "black markets". There is therefore, a basic tendency to liberalise imports. Once these contradictions are taken into account, the balance of payments crisis of the mid-1960s and the subsequent deceleration in industrial growth, are explained.

The 1980s' Turnaround

Seen in this light, what was surprising was not the industrial impasse of the mid-1960s but the turnaround in industrial growth in the 1980s. The decade of the 1980s witnessed a recovery and even acceleration of industrial growth and manufacturing activity. This return to economic buoyancy cannot be attributed to the emergence of any new source of stimulus to growth. Exports during these years were, by no means remarkable enough to stimulate growth in an economy as large as that of India. And the factors which had earlier constrained the expansion of the mass market were still operating. This implied that the stimulus to growth, as before, had to come from the state.

And this is essentially what happened. There were three new features which characterised the 1980s, which allowed the economy to escape from the growth impasse of the earlier period. First, there was a big increase in the fiscal stimulus to the economy, provided by government spending. Second, there was substantial liberalisation of imports, especially of capital goods and components for manufacturing. Third, associated with both of these, there was a shift to relying on external commercial borrowing, by the state, to finance the increases in the consequent fiscal and current account deficits.

In sum, the turnaround in the mid-1980s was a result of the ability of the Indian government to leverage external finance, to drive growth into the system. The question that arises then is why the Indian government and the capitalist class were not able to do this earlier. The answer to this question takes us to developments outside the country, which influenced India's medium-term growth prospects significantly. Principal among these developments, was the rise to dominance of finance capital in the international economy. The major historical landmarks in the latter process are worth recalling. Till the early 1970s, the private international financial system played only a limited role in recycling financial surpluses to the developing countries. Capital flows to developing countries, barring a few unusual exceptions like South Korea, were through official bilateral and multilateral channels. The period immediately after the first oil shock saw a dramatic change in this scenario. Since oil surpluses were held in the main as deposits with the international banking system controlled by the developed world, the private financial system there became a powerful agent for recycling surpluses. This power was indeed immense. Expenditure fuelled by credit in the developed and developing world, generated surpluses with the oil producers, who deposited these surpluses with the transnational banks, who, in turn, could offer further doses of credit. By 1981, OPEC countries are estimated to have accumulated surpluses in the tune of $475 billion, $400 billion of which was parked in the developed industrial nations.

Two other developments contributed to the increase in international liquidity during the 1970s and 1980s. First, the United States had built up large international liabilities during the Bretton Woods years, including those resulting from expenditures on the Vietnam War and its policing efforts elsewhere in the world. The explosion of the Euro currency market in the 1970s reflected this. This was sustained by the confidence in the dollar, stemming from the immediate post-War hegemony of the US, which made it as good as gold. Such international confidence in its currency allowed the US to ignore national budget constraints on its international spending and resulted in the emergence of strong banking and financial interests, with an international agenda. The influence of these interests was reflected in policies that affected domestic manufacturing interests adversely, as reflected in the widening and persistent US trade deficit after the mid-1970s.

Second, there was a change in demographic structure in most of the advanced countries, with the post-War baby boomers generation reaching the age when they would emphasise personal savings for retirement. This resulted in growing demands for more variety in savings instruments as well as higher returns, leading to the greater significance of pension funds, mutual funds and the like.

One consequence of these trends was an increase in the international assets of the big banks of the developed world. This trend has gained strength in recent years. In mid-1997, the international asset position of banks resident in 23 countries stood at $9.95 trillion. By June 2007, when 40 countries were reporting, this had risen to $33.71 trillion, with external assets totalling $29.98 trillion. The reasons are obvious. Since bank profits depend on the spread between the interest they pay their depositors and the interest they charge their lenders, when deposits with banks grow, their lending must expand. Initially this lending was within the developed world itself. But soon, that was not enough. As a result, developing countries which were earlier considered too risky to lend to or invest in, were rediscovered as "emerging markets" by the international banks and some among them were offered capital flows if they chose to open their economies. India began exploiting that opportunity in the 1980s, in the form of external commercial borrowing, leading to a change in its relationship with international finance.

That change was not without its problems. Exploiting the access to foreign exchange, the government resorted to a fiscal stimulus, financed with borrowing. The demand stimulus resulting from such expenditure was serviced by the domestic industry with the help of imported capital goods, intermediates and raw materials, imports of which were liberalised. This essentially meant that the import intensity of domestic production rose. But such growth was not constrained by inadequate access to foreign exchange, since it was accompanied by an increase in foreign borrowing from the IMF, the international commercial banking system and remittances from non-resident Indians. India's foreign debt to GDP ratio doubled during the 1980s. It was when international creditors chose to shut off such credit at the end of the 1980s that India ran into the balance of payments crisis of 1990-91, which provided the grounds for the advocates of reform to go in for an IMF-style stabilisation and adjustment strategy.

A New Phase

It was after this crisis that India entered the second phase of its relationship with international finance, when the role of other forms of capital flow, especially financial investments in equity markets, became extremely important. To facilitate such flows, regulatory controls on such flows were substantially diluted or even dismantled. As a result, in the period between 1993 and 2003, there was an increase, though moderate, in the average volume of capital inflows. But, after 2003 there has been a veritable surge in the inflow. The perception of India as an "emerging economic power" in the global system derives whatever strength it has from the developments during the last five to six years because India, like other emerging markets, has been the chosen destination for investment, from the centres of international finance. In the recent years, India has emerged as a leader among these markets.

There has been an extraordinary surge in foreign institutional investments since April 2003. Such investments, which averaged $1776 million a year during 1993-94 to 1997-98, dipped to an average of $295 million during 1997-99, rose again to $1829 million during 1999-2000 to 2001-02 only to fall to $377 million in 2002-03. The surge began thereafter. Inflows averaged $9800 million a year during 2003-06, slumped in 2006-07 and are estimated at $20,328 million during 2007-08. While cumulative net FII inflows into India, since the liberalisation of rules governing such inflows, in the early 1990s till end-March 2003, amounted to $15,635 million, the increment in the cumulative value between that date and the end of March 2008, was $57,860 million.

These recent developments point to a qualitative change in India's relationship with international finance. Until the late 1990s, India relied on capital inflows to cover deficits in foreign exchange needed to finance its current transactions, because foreign exchange earned through exports and received as remittances, fell substantially short of the amount needed to pay for imports, interest and dividends. However, since India has been receiving excess capital, it has been forced to export them, not because accumulated foreign exchange reserves need to be invested, but because it is seeking alternative ways of absorbing the excess capital that flows into the country.

Policy has had a major role in this. Underlying the current FII surge is, of course, a continuous process of liberalisation of the rules, governing such investments: its sources, its ambit, the caps it was subject to and the tax laws pertaining to it. It is well recognised that stock market buoyancy and volatility has been a phenomenon typical of the liberalisation years.

It could, however, be argued that while the process of liberalisation began in the early 1990s, the surge in foreign investment is a relatively new phenomenon which must be related to the returns now available to the investors that make it worth their while to exploit the opportunity offered by liberalisation. The point, however, is that access to FIIs has been widened considerably in recent times and returns on stock market investment have been hiked through state policy, adopted as part of the reform. As per the September 1992 policy permitting foreign institutional investment, registered FIIs could individually invest a maximum of 5 per cent of the company's issued capital and all FIIs together, up to a maximum of 24 per cent. The 5 per cent individual-FII limit was raised to 10 per cent in June 1998. However, as of March 2001, FIIs as a group, were allowed to invest in excess of 24 per cent and up to 40 per cent of the paid up capital of a company, with the approval of the general body of the shareholders granted through a special resolution. This aggregate FII limit was linked to sectoral cap in September 2001. In many sectors, the FDI cap has been increased to 100 per cent. These changes obviously substantially expanded the role that FIIs can play even in a market that is still relatively shallow in terms of the number of shares that are available for active trading.

But it was not merely the flexibility, provided to FIIs to hold a high proportion of equity in domestic companies, that was responsible for the stock market surge. The latter was partly engineered too. Just before the FII surge began, and influenced, perhaps by the sharp fall in the net FII investments in 2002-03, the then Finance Minister declared in the Budget for 2003-04: "In order to give a further fillip to the capital markets, it is now proposed to exempt all listed equities that were acquired on or after March 1, 2003, and sold after the lapse of a year, or more, from the incidence of capital gains tax. Long term capital gains tax will, therefore, not hereafter apply to such transactions. This proposal should facilitate investment in equities." Long term capital gains tax was being levied at the rate of 10 per cent up to that point of time. The surge was, no doubt, facilitated by this significant concession.

What needs to be noted is that the very next year, the Finance Minister of the UPA government endorsed this move. In his 2004 budget speech, he announced his decision to "abolish the tax on long-term capital gains from securities transactions altogether." Thus, an extravagant fiscal concession appears to have triggered the speculative surge in the stock market that continues to persist.

The Problem of Volatility

Given the presence of foreign institutional investors and their active trading behaviour, small and periodic shifts in their behaviour lead to market volatility. Such volatility is an inevitable result of the structure of India's financial markets as well. Markets in developing countries like India are thin or shallow in at least three senses. First, only stocks of a few companies are actively traded in the market. Thus, although there are more than 8000 companies listed on the stock exchange, the BSE Sensex incorporates just 30 companies, trading in whose shares is seen as an indicative of market activity. Second, of these stocks, there is only a small proportion that is routinely available for trading, while the rest are held by promoters, the financial institutions and others interested in corporate control or influence. And third, the number of players trading in these stocks,0) is also small. According to the Annual Report of the Securities and Exchange Board of India for 1999-2000, shares of only around 40 per cent of the listed companies were being traded. Further: "Trading is only on a nominal basis in quite a large number of companies, which is reflected from the fact that companies in which trading took place for 1 to 10 trade days during 1999-2000, constituted nearly 56 per cent of 8020 companies or nearly 65 per cent of companies were traded for 1 to 40 days. Only 23 per cent were traded for 100 days and above. Thus, it would be seen that during the year under review, a major portion of the companies was hardly traded." (SEBI 2000: 85). The net impact is that speculation and volatility are essential features of such markets.

These features of Indian stock markets induce a high degree of volatility for four reasons. Inasmuch as an increase in investment by FIIs triggers a sharp price increase, it would provide additional incentives for FII investment and in the first instance encourage further purchases, so that there is a tendency for any correction of price increases to be delayed. And when the correction begins, it would have to be led by an FII pull-out and can take the form of an extremely sharp decline in prices.

Secondly, as and when FIIs are attracted to the market by expectations of a price increase that tend to be automatically realised, the inflow of foreign capital can result in an appreciation of the rupee vis-à-vis the dollar (say). This increases the return earned in foreign exchange, when rupee assets are sold and the revenue converted into dollars. As a result, the investments turn even more attractive, triggering an investment spiral that would imply a sharper fall when any correction begins.

Thirdly, the growing realisation by the FIIs, of the power they wield in what are shallow markets, encourages speculative investment aimed at pushing the market up and choosing an appropriate moment to exit. This implicit manipulation of the market, if resorted to often enough, would obviously imply a substantial increase in volatility.

Finally, in volatile markets, domestic speculators too attempt to manipulate markets in periods of unusually high prices.

Possible Ripple Effects

These aspects of the market are of significance because financial liberalisation has meant that developments in equity markets can have major repercussions elsewhere too in the system. With banks allowed to play a greater role in equity markets, any slump in those markets can affect the functioning of parts of the banking system. For example, the forced closure (through merger with Punjab National Bank) of one bank (Nedungadi Bank) was the result of the losses it suffered because of over exposure in the stock market.

On the other hand, if any set of developments encourages an unusually high outflow of FII capital from the market, it can adversely impact the value of the rupee and set off speculation in the currency market that can, in special circumstances, result in a currency crisis. There are now, too many instances, of such effects worldwide for it to be dismissed on the ground that India's reserves are adequate enough to manage such situations.

Financial Flows and Fiscal Contraction

The growing presence of FIIs is disconcerting not just because such flows are in the nature of "hot money" which renders the external sector fragile, but because the effort to attract such flows and manage any surge in such flows, that may occur, has a number of macroeconomic implications. Most importantly, inasmuch as financial liberalisation leads to financial growth and increases the presence and role of financial agents in the economy, it forces the state to adopt a deflationary stance to appease financial interests. Those interests are against deficit-financed spending by the state, for a number of reasons. First, deficit financing is seen to increase the liquidity overhang in the system, and therefore as being potentially inflationary. Inflation is anathema to finance since it erodes the real value of financial assets. Second, since government spending is "autonomous" in character, the use of debt to finance such autonomous spending is seen as introducing into financial markets, an arbitrary player, not driven by profit motive, whose activities can render interest rate differentials that determine financial profits more unpredictable. Third, if deficit spending leads to a substantial build-up of the state's debt and interest burden, it may intervene in financial markets to lower interest rates with implications for financial returns. Financial interests wanting to guard against that possibility tend to oppose deficit spending. Finally, the use of deficit spending to support autonomous expenditures by the state, amounts to an implicit legitimisation of an interventionist state, and therefore, a de-legitimisation of the market. Since global finance seeks to de-legitimise the state and legitimise the market, it strongly opposes deficit-financed, autonomous state spending.

Efforts to curb the deficit inevitably involve a contraction of public expenditure, especially expenditure on capital formation, which adversely affects growth and employment; leads to a curtailment of social sector expenditures that sets back the battle against deprivation; impacts adversely food and other subsidies that benefit the poor; and sets off a scramble to privatise profit-earning public assets, which render the self-imposed fiscal strait-jacket, self-perpetuating. All the more so, since the finance-induced pressure to limit deficit spending is institutionalised through legislation, like the Fiscal Responsibility and Budget Management Act passed in 2004 in India, which constitutionally binds the state to do away with revenue deficits and limit fiscal deficits to low, pre-specified levels.

Cause for Concern

All this has, however, not received the attention it deserves because the liquidity in the Indian economy, resulting from the capital surge, has helped sustain a credit-financed, private expenditure-based process of growth in the economy. Credit financed purchases of housing, automobiles, durables and ordinary goods and services has driven growth to near 9 per cent levels for the last few years, barring the period of the Great Recession. With GDP figures touching 9 per cent growth, little attention has also been paid to a disconcerting feature of India's external payments position. Taking a long view, we find that the current account deficit on the balance of payments which fell from 3.4 per cent of GDP in crisis year 1990-91 to 0.6 per cent in 2000-01 (and even turned to surplus in the subsequent three years) has now widened from a marginal 0.4 per cent of GDP in 2004-05 to 3.3 per cent in 2009-10. This widening of the current deficit, is on account of two factors. First, the merchandise trade deficit in India's external account has risen from 2.3 per cent of GDP in 2002-03 to 10 per cent in 2009-10. And, second, the year 2009-10 has seen a sudden decline in revenues from services, which fell from 4.6 per cent of GDP to 2.9 per cent of GDP. Matters would have been much worse if remittances, as reflected in the Private Transfers figure, had not remained at high levels.

It is true that in the short run, these developments need not provide much cause for worry since India is once again receiving inflows of foreign capital, that far exceed what is needed to finance its current account deficit. Foreign exchange reserves too are in excess of $280 billion, providing more than an adequate buffer. There is no fear whatsoever of a 1991-style balance of payments crisis.

But the figures do point to a long term syndrome that must colour the otherwise bright picture of the country's economic performance. Ever since India opted for its first big IMF loan in 1981, in the aftermath of the second oil shock, increased dependence on foreign capital inflows has been justified on the grounds that they provide India with the wherewithal to transform its economic structure and redress what is its long-term weakness: poor export performance. Capital flows, it was argued, would: (i) allow the country to liberalise trade and subject domestic economic agents to efficiency-enhancing international competition; (ii) permit Indian firms to access the foreign exchange, needed to import the capital and technology required to modernise their equipment and establish internationally competitive capacities that would allow them to compete in export markets; (iii) bring with them international producers, intent on using India as a base and source for production for the world market; and (iv) finance any "interim" deficit that may result from an import surge that follows trade liberalisation but precedes India's transformation into a successful exporter.

What the long-term tendency in the merchandise trade deficit indicates is that close to two decades after the programme of accelerated liberalisation was adopted, these expectations have remained unrealised. India has been successful as an exporter of workers who send back remittances and as an exporter of services of various kinds, but has failed miserably in its original effort to become a hub for the export of manufactures. In fact, periods when the merchandise trade deficit was low, were ones in which low growth or recessionary conditions were resulting in curtailed imports rather than years in which exports were booming. It was only because of the country's "invisible" income from remittances and services that the current account deficit for much of this period was kept low. Yet the deficit implies that India's comfortable foreign reserves are borrowed and not earned.

The period from 2004-05, when India moved on to a high growth trajectory (between 8 and 9 per cent) is a period when the merchandise trade deficit has widened quite sharply. This did not matter too much till recently, since remittance incomes were sustained, while incomes from the exports of miscellaneous services (including, IT, IT-enabled and business services) were rising significantly. It was when the latter dipped in 2009-10 that the current deficit widened to levels that could be a cause for concern.

The change is of concern also because of the likelihood that remittance incomes may also dip. It has been known for long that the Gulf countries (which fall in the "Sterling area") are no more the principal or dominant source of remittances. Since the mid-1990s, that position has been acquired by countries in the "Dollar area", especially the United States. This is because of the rising volume of remittances from temporary workers on H1 B visas, who move for relatively short periods to deliver services on site, in the United States. The recent controversy over the H1 B visa fee, which has been doubled, indicates that official hostility to such workers may be on the rise and on site service delivery is likely to prove more expensive. If that results in a dip in remittances from the dollar area even while higher growth increases India's import bill and widens its merchandise trade deficit, the current account deficit could become even larger. That may then give actual cause for concern and affect even India's position as a favoured destination for the foreign investors. There is no visible crisis here, but a worrisome weakness maybe.

Sanjay Baru

Recent Trends in the Indian Economy

The modern history of Indian economic development begins with India's Independence in 1947. The six decades since then can be divided into three distinct phases. The first phase from 1947 to 1980 was marked by relatively modest growth, compared to several other newly industrialising economies of Asia, with the average rate of growth being around 3.5 per cent per year. The second phase of development, from 1980 to 2000, saw an acceleration of economic growth, with the average rate of growth being around 6.0 per cent. The important turning point of the second phase was 1991, when a series of economic reform measures helped stabilise the economy, improve India's external economic and fiscal profile. The third phase begins around 2000, after the dotcom boom and bust, with a new phase of private sector led growth culminating in India recording almost 9.0 per cent growth for a continuous period of five years, from 2003-08.

For the first three decades following independence, India consciously sought to build a mixed economy. One of the main objectives of economic policy was to redress the weaknesses inherent in a developing economy with a poor capital and infrastructural base. State intervention and investment were justified on the grounds of 'private investment failure'. The Second Five-Year Plan (195560) witnessed heavy public investment in the core industrial sector as well as in transport and communications. While this was politically advertised as being the basis for the building of a 'socialistic pattern of society', in reality, public investment, both in industry and agriculture, was supplemented by private investment, which laid the foundations for the growth of indigenous business enterprise.

India's protected industrial sector thrived during the first half of the 1960s. However, a series of poor monsoons, two wars with Pakistan (in 1965 and 1971) and rising social and political discontent curbed productive investment, leading to a deceleration in the rate of growth of industrial production, throughout the 1970s. In order to adjust to this low-growth phase and in response to pressures from new business groups (both domestic and non-resident Indians), a series of policy changes were carried out, liberalising the highly regulated economy and making production for exports, rather than for the internal market, relatively profitable. The first phase of this new liberal economic policy was introduced in 1978-80. The rise in the cost of petroleum on the world market in 1979, however, forced the Government to revert to a more regulated economy. The second phase of economic liberalisation was implemented during the early months of Rajiv Gandhi's premiership (1985-1989).

Compared with the low economic growth rate of the 1970s (with an average annual GDP growth rate of 3.5 per cent), the 1980s witnessed moderate to high growth, with an average annual GDP growth rate of 5.5 per cent. This increase was largely due to a steep rise in public expenditure and investment. The modest liberalisation of the import regime facilitated access to new technologies, which, in turn, encouraged expansion in the consumer durables, electronics and petrochemicals industries. The Government had not, however, protected itself against an excessive level of borrowing, both domestically and internationally. India's excellent sovereign credit rating allowed it easy access to global financial markets in the late 1980s, and both long and short-term debts were rapidly accumulated.

Given the high accumulation of debt and the concomitant burden of debt servicing, and in the absence of an adequate growth in exports, India found itself unable to withstand the adverse effects of the Gulf crisis in mid-1990. Partly on account of this and partly on account of the poor political assessments of credit-rating agencies, which believed that a minority Government would be unable to pursue policies that would stabilise the Indian economy, India's credit rating began to slip, in the latter half of 1990. Faced with the risk of default, the Government imposed draconian import control measures, borrowed extensively from the IMF and, in July 1991, devalued the rupee by 20 per cent.

The balance-of-payments crisis of mid-1991 coincided with the arrival in office, of a new Congress Party Government, led by Prime Minister P. V.

Narasimha Rao, with the former Governor of the Reserve Bank of India, Dr Manmohan Singh, as Minister of Finance. The Rao-Singh team utilised the opportunity opened by the payments crisis, to make the Indian economy more accessible to foreign trade and investment flows. Implementing a traditional structural adjustment programme, designed with the assistance of the World Bank and the IMF, India liberalised its trade and investment policies, announced a programme of fiscal stabilisation, aimed at reducing the fiscal deficit from more than 8.5 per cent of GDP to 5.0 per cent, initiated a policy for phasing out short-term external debt exposure and reduced the current-account deficit from more than 3.0 per cent of GDP to less than 2.0 per cent, within a year. Along with this medium-term adjustment and stabilisation programme, the Government gradually introduced extensive changes in industrial and tax policies.

The policies to transform the Indian economy from an inward-orientated, import-substituting model of industrial development to an outward-orientated model were further developed by successive governments, throughout the 1990s. As a result, the policies not only prevented external default, but also helped to increase India's foreign-exchange assets several-fold within a short period of time. There was a sharp decrease in both fiscal and current-account deficits and an improvement in the external debt profile. The rise in reserves in the mid-1990s, coincided with India's opening of its stock market to investment by foreign institutional investors, such as pension and mutual funds. India's recovery from a balance-of-payments crisis is regarded as one of the fastest achieved under an IMF-World Bank adjustment and stabilisation programme. In part, the success of the Indian strategy lay in the ability of the authorities to ensure relative freedom from the IMF-World Bank orthodoxy, in order to pursue an unorthodox and unconventional approach to fiscal and balance-of-payments correction. As well as stabilising the economy, these policies also helped to accelerate the rate of growth of the Indian economy. Compared with the long-term annual rate of growth of around 4.0 per cent during 1950-90, the Indian economy was able to register an average rate of growth of more than 5.7 per cent per year in the period 1992-2008, with annual growth averaging 8.8 per cent in 2003-

08.

According to the UN Development Programme's Human Development Report 2007, India's human development indicators showed an improvement in the 1990s. India, once considered a country with 'low' human development, has advanced to the category of 'medium' human development. According to the report's estimates of the Human Development Index (HDI), India ranked 128 in a list of 177 countries. These estimates of HDI, however, were based on the profile in 2005. While India's HDI did rise during the 1990s, the increasingly widening gap between the country's HDI and per caput GDP ranking in the 'negative direction' has been a worrying phenomenon. According to the Human Development Report 2007, India's position in terms of per caput GDP was 11 places higher than its ranking in terms of HDI, indicating that the country could do much better in distributing the benefits of its GDP growth. Until the late 1990s, there was little difference between India's HDI and per caput GDP rank.

Challenges Ahead

The rapid acceleration in Indian economic growth in the early years of the 21st century has changed global impressions of India. Indian companies have made their mark in the world marketplace in a number of fields, from consumer products to sophisticated engineering and IT services; Indian professionals are much sought after in numerable services, of which computer software is only one; Indian exports have been growing at a rate of more than 20 per cent per year; and the country has emerged as the preferred global location for the provision of low-cost services. India is no longer seen as a poor economy that has consistently under-fulfilled its potential. Instead, it is now seen as a new driving force in the global economy, one that rivals China in the changing international balance of economic power.

The Indian economy has grown by more than 5 per cent per year since the early 1980s. However, the acceleration to an 8 per cent or more growth rate took place only during the first decade of the 21st century, an average of 8.8 per cent growth per year between 2003/04 and 2007/08, compared with an average of 5.4 per cent growth per year over the previous five years (1998/99 -2002/03). This acceleration prompted the Planning

Commission of the Indian Government, to set a target of average annual growth of 9 per cent, during the 11th Five-Year Plan (2007/08 - 2011/12).

The global economic slowdown, following the trans-Atlantic financial crisis, did have an impact on the Indian economy, albeit a modest one, given India's relatively low share in global trade and capital flows. In 2008/09 India's growth rate slipped to 6.7 per cent, after four years of 9.0 per cent growth. This was still a substantial pace of expansion, but the export sector and Indian manufacturing suffered a major slowdown and even contraction. India experienced a surge in food prices in early 2008 (in line with the global trend) and also had to cope with the rise in international crude oil prices (which kept increasing until July). Both increases pushed inflation in wholesale prices to more than 12 per cent in August. However, the bigger impact was that of the global financial crisis, which unfolded from September 2008 onwards and turned into a full fledged recession towards the end of the year. Indian companies found that their credit lines had dried up. As global trade collapsed, India's exports also declined drastically. Domestic investment decelerated and manufacturing growth too decreased sharply. The one major adverse impact that India avoided was a deterioration of the financial sector. Thanks to the RBI's policy of caution and its curbs on adopting the more risky practices, there were no serious problems in the banking sector, and India was one of the few countries in the world to be able to withstand the financial crisis. This enabled India to become an active member of the newly created Group of 20 (G-20) heads of government summit. India's economist Prime Minister, Manmohan Singh played an active role at G-20 summits in Washington, London, Pittsburgh and Toronto, urging leaders of developed countries, to sustain expansionary macroeconomic policies that would enable global growth to rise and create new employment and trade opportunities.

The description of India as having arrived on the global scene is as incomplete as the earlier characterisation of the country, as an underdeveloped and backward economy. The acceleration in GDP growth in 2003-07 to more than 8 per cent per year is, of course, a continuation of a two-decade old process of improvement. The increase in India's rate of economic growth began in the early 1980s, although it was only in the early years of the first decade of the 2000s, that the economy appeared ready to climb to new heights of growth. While there is little denying the acceleration in the rate of growth, a number of issues are regularly posed in India on various aspects of the new momentum, all of which relate to its quality and sustainability. Of especial concern in the midst of the acceleration in economic growth, are the sharp divisions in the economy which have been accentuated since the 1990s. There are many facets to these divisions. There are the increasing regional disparities: growth in southern, western and parts of northern India has accelerated, but it has slowed down in many states in central, eastern and other parts of northern India. The latter group of regions contain the bulk of the population and a predominant majority of the country's poor, implying that inequalities have grown and economic benefits have been distributed unequally. There are also the sectoral disparities. The service sector and, to a lesser extent, the manufacturing sector have performed well since the 1990s, but the agricultural sector, which still employs nearly three-fifths of the work-force, has seen a deceleration in its growth rate and widespread discontent among the farming community. This is reflected in the rural-urban divide, with the cities and towns showing an economic dynamism and rural India experiencing considerable economic difficulties. Yet another divide is apparent within the cities themselves, with the poor and marginalised (many of them migrants from the rural areas) being pushed to the outer fringes of the urban centres and being denied basic facilities, while the city centres and suburbs begin to mirror the more prosperous urban locations elsewhere in the world. All these disparities are expressed with the general unease that rapid growth has not been broadly based. There is an awareness across the political spectrum that uneven economic expansion is not sustainable.

In the light of such an uneven spread of the gains from rapid growth it has become apparent, at least internally, that focussing only on some areas of success and transformation does not provide a complete picture of the Indian economy today. The IT sector is growing in leaps and bounds, but, although it employs more than 2 million young men and women, this still constitutes just a small fraction of the Indian labour force of 400m. A true transformation of the Indian economy will take place only when the manufacturing and agricultural sectors enjoy the same degree of success as the IT sector.

In the parliamentary elections held in May 2009, the UPA Government was returned to power on the promise of promoting 'inclusive' growth. The mandate was seen as an endorsement of government policies, which, over the previous five years, had sought to combine rapid growth, with a substantial increase in expenditure on welfare programmes. The latter was intended to reduce disparities and spread growth more evenly. Foremost among the welfare programmes was the National Rural Employment Guarantee Scheme which promised one member of every eligible household in the rural areas, 100 days of employment in a public-works programme. Although, since its inauguration in 2005, this mammoth programme has not proved entirely successful, it has, neveretheless, made a difference to the poorest households in India's villages. On reassuming power in June 2009, the new Government reiterated its resolve to pursue inclusive growth. This would involve expanding programmes, targeted at the deprived and vulnerable, in both rural and urban India, while simultaneously restoring the growth momentum that had declined with the onset of the global recession.

In its first year in office, the government, headed by Prime Minister Manmohan Singh, had focussed on sustaining higher economic growth while seeking to secure control over inflation. While the government aimed for 9.0 per cent growth with 5.0 per cent inflation, in 2010, it saw 8.0 per cent growth with 8.0 per cent average inflation. Reducing inflation, while pushing growth up, and ensuring that the current account deficit remains at around 3.0 per cent of GDP, is the most important economic challenge for India's macroeconomic authorities. In the longer run, however, India needs a strategy for generating employment in the non-farm, manufacturing sector, that will enable her to deal with the challenge of landlessness and poverty in rural areas and the reduced share of agriculture in national income.

The key to India sustaining her current high rates of growth, lies in the economy and the polity's ability to promote broad-based, labour-intensive industrialisation.

Kamal Nayan Kabra

Employment in Neo-liberalised India: Some Theoretical and Empirical Issues

The most direct way of raising lowest incomes is to raise the zero incomes of the unemployed ... Employment is intimately related to technology both quantitatively and qualitatively. The third world urgently needs more jobs ... Qualitative aspects of employment such as efficiency or satisfying work are luxuries for nations, rich enough to have achieved almost full employment. In the third world, employment of any kind is an advance over no employment since it provides income, however modest. Creating employment is therefore the best way to reduce poverty." --- J. Tinbergen (1979) in 'Activities to Promote Appropriate Technology' in "Conceptual and Policy Framework for Appropriate Industrial Technology," UNIDO, UN, New York, pp. 36-37.

"It may be better to allow machines to remain idle rather than to keep human beings unemployed." --- PC Mahalanobis (1955) in 'The Approach of Operational Research to Planning in India,' "Sankhya", 16, Part I.

"To reduce unemployment is to remove one of the main causes of poverty and inequality. A reduction in inequality will of course reduce poverty ceteris paribus." --- D. Seers (1979), 'The Meaning of Development' in "Development Theory: Four Critical Studies."

"The basic weakness in our employment performance is the failure of the Indian economy to create a sufficient volume of additional high quality employment to absorb the new entrants into the labour force while also facilitating the absorption of surplus labour that currently exists in the agricultural sector, into higher wage, on-agricultural employment. A successful transition to inclusive growth (clearly it is admitted that whatever we have had so far is far from inclusive) is migration of such surplus workers to other areas for productive and gainful employment in the organised or unorganised sector." --- Eleventh Five Year Plan, 2007-12, Volume I, Inclusive Growth, p.63

Introduction

The present exercise intends to examine some select aspects of the employment situation in India as it has evolved during the last two decades of neo-liberal policies. To begin with, we raise some questions regarding the compatibility of the neo-liberal policies with the quest for regular productive work, to enable every adult to acquire, over a visible time horizon, at least an acceptable minimum of the means to satisfy the needs, that living in a society, creates. This is followed by an attempt to examine some of the available evidence regarding the way these policies impacted the employment situation, in its different aspects. The last part attempts simultaneously to examine the role specific policies, played in order to lead us to the prevailing employment challenge as also to point towards some means to improve the outcomes, in directions consistent with the objective of an exclusion-free society.

It may be mentioned as a matter of overall perspective, that our analysis finds another set of disturbingly powerful empirical co-relatives from a major third world country that is India - a country that took pioneering initiatives among the newly liberalised countries, towards evolving a welfare state way back in early 1950s (decorated of course with socialistic verbiage as that was in a way the hey day of various brands of socialism on the global scene) for stressing the imperative of moving towards fuller employment for her teeming millions - that underscores the great truth of Karl Polanyi's proposition that for liberalism, no price is too high for economic improvement. The tragedy for the Indian masses, struggling against the great odd of livelihood inadequacy and insecurity, the essence of unemployment, consists of the fact that neither the ruling elites nor the dominant theories and ideologies, recognised steady movement towards gainful and assured employment, to be the essence of economic improvement. Even to this day, the tragedy perpetrated by intellectual conmanship and democratic-political deceit, persists in various forms as even after the demonstrated inability of high and largely continuously attained growth of GDP, the livelihood crisis staring the people at every step of their lives, continues to get worse.

I

Third World Employment/Unemployment Problem under Neo-liberalism

It is generally believed and is a verifiable fact that a commitment to ensure adequate and secure livelihoods for every one, over a reasonable period of time, as a matter of enforceable right and hence one of the key elements, enjoying a high public policy priority (something that follows from the pursuit of democratic, all-round development) forms no part of the agenda of the globally practiced neo-liberal policy package. On the contrary, an official publication of the government of India clearly states that "Asking the government to produce all the essential goods, create all the necessary jobs, and keep a curb on the prices of all goods is to, at best, court failure" (Economic Survey, 2009-10, GOI, Ministry of Finance, p.22). Actually, it has been shown that the real agenda pursued by means of neo-liberalisation is to restore and maintain the conditions for continued and sustained capital accumulation by and under the hegemony of the organised private capital, both nationally and globally, by using both the market and state processes and whatever else it takes (D. Harvey, 2010, Chapters 2 & 3). Of course, one would come across plenty of ex-cathedra statements and writings, by scholars of neo-liberal persuasion, maintaining at the time of the initiation of the 'project neo-liberalisation' that the faster pace of economic growth, resulting from the unfreezing of the market forces and moving towards globalisation of the economic and market processes in the Third World countries (TWCs), are essential for increasing, inter alia, 'employment' as an observable outcome. As the quotation from the 11th Plan at the beginning of the paper states, a process of disillusionment has set in. The planners in India go on to factor in a fact of considerable salience in so far as they state that "the problem is heightened by the fact that the relatively higher rate of growth achieved during the last decade or so is not seen to generate a sufficient volume of good quality employment." However, the planners are not seen to make it clear in the Plan, whether this outcome is a contingent, transient factor or something basic, long-term and substantive.

Notwithstanding such ambivalence over the approach towards livelihood issues, there seems to prevail, a broad consensus that making adequate and assured livelihood opportunities available to everyone is the most daunting and widely appreciated challenge that poor TWCs, such as India, face. They face this challenge not only presently but this has been the case over a long historical period of their existence, including the era of their direct colonial subjugation. Surely the neo-liberals would not quite go with the formulation in such a form and with such an emphasis but the essence of what is implied by it is unlikely to be denied by them, in so far as the problem of mass scale and chronic unemployment, is universally recognised as a serious issue. However, the neo-liberal theories define and specify the problem, largely in ways that are similar to or fashioned after the exposition of the problem of unemployment in the rich, industrialised market economies that experience cyclical fluctuations. While the rich industrialised countries face unemployment as a cyclical issue, the TWCs face it as a structural, endemic problem, that arose as a legacy of the historical experience of colonial domination and its impact on the indigenous socio-economic structures and processes

Given the limited size of the organised labour market in the latter group of countries, there arises the need to comprehend the employment question, with a different conceptual and theoretical tool box. Hence one has to take note of the fact that the neo-liberals follow the practice prevalent in the mainstream economics of development, that spells out the problem of employment in terms of a variety of concepts, theories and measurements that have little direct relationship with livelihood adequacy and insecurity as such (for a recent exposition of such a perspective, dealing specifically with the Indian situation see, World Bank, 2010). Given the lack of appreciation of the livelihood - work opportunities linkage, it is not surprising that, this approach does not relate unemployment to closely related issues of poverty and inequalities and to the broader basic question of endemic, mass social exclusion [See K.N. Kabra, 2010, Social Exclusion: The basic Problematic of the Third World Countries, Professor H.S. Pradhan Memorial Lecture at the A.N. Sinha Institute, Patna (forthcoming)].

The neo-liberal approach essentially identifies employment in terms of the subjective perception of a person whether she/he considers herself/himself employed or not and the extent of one's employment. Whether such engagement/participation in labour processes, under diverse organisational frameworks and associated conditions of engagement, go with some objective social criteria of acquiring access to certain common and objectively specified threshold of regular and adequate flows of income, while contributing to the overall social kitty of flow of goods and services, does not seem to enter the concept of employment, used by the neo-liberal theories. Trying to capture the factual position, regarding people's participation in the economic activities during a period of time or at a point of time, making clear cut or identifiable contribution that entitles them to a reward for it, that is, attempts at finding out the occupational status of the people, mainly the adults, as participants in the economic processes, on terms and in forms that are the common currency in a country, requires the application of some common parameters and their uniform and consistent application. No doubt, it is a daunting task that requires regular monitoring throughout the country and sporadic attempts to gather such information would rarely be able to capture the reality. No subjective perceptions-based information collected on the basis of periodic economy-wide field sample surveys can prove equal to the task, as outlined above. They would later, possibly throw up various measures of employment / unemployment, that cannot capture, in an objective manner, the actual place of the people, in the economic and social landscape, their relative and absolute position and the level, growth and sustainability of their well-being and contribution to national level economic variables. These data about the people treated as employed or unemployed in various senses and to varying degrees, based on the respondents' own perception, fail to say much and consistently about their place and prospects in social networks and hierarchies, or the substance and sustainability of such 'employment' opportunities. These are among the factors that make the aggregation of such subjective responses, lack objectivity, credibility, comparability and usability for devising effective policies that can effectively make the deprivation and exclusion, entailed by lack or inadequacy of employment opportunities' history, over a reasonable time horizon. One need not prolong the discussion of the inadequacies and inappropriateness of the ways of making sense of and measuring the nature and extent of employment. It seems that the subjective perceptions-based aggregation of employment level has become a part and parcel of the neo-liberal approach to gauging and identifying the nature and extent of employment, in so far as moving towards an adequate and assured level of livelihood, satisfying a common threshold, forms no part of the criteria of effectiveness that a neo-liberal approach sets for itself or that is accepted as a commonly understood task of any economy. These limitations and inadequacies of the commonly prevalent measures of employment/unemployment have lately found acceptance in many official reports too (For a detailed critique of the conventional measures of employment, see, NCEUS, 2010).

After all, in the fundamentalist orthodoxy of market and growth, a low priority and limited salience is given to the problem of employment as a by-product of the production decisions, based on individual perspective of the investors. That is something deeply embedded in the political economy of neo-liberalism. It is not concerned directly with the issues like whether such so-called employment enables one to meet his/her basic needs and also make some reckonable contribution to social output flows (what matters is the net positive gain that an employer is able to make, by agreeing to pay a certain level of wages and the level of employment would be stretched up to the level, where the net gain from hiring an additional hand becomes zero). Thus if one considers oneself employed, so be it. The level of reward is for the market forces to decide. As for its security of tenure, the neo-liberals make the level of hiring dependent, inter alia, on the ease with which firing can be done by the hirers, at their discretion. Thus, in this perspective, it is only individuals and families that exist, employment issue comes to its own when the aggregate effective demand falls short of the aggregate supply and causes involuntary unemployment. Then, of course, the Keynesian remedies, not ordinarily favoured by the neo-liberals, come to be adopted, by the state.

Be as it may, one thing is clear - at the level of popular masses, the question of employment is a real life and death issue and hardly any other issue can compete with it for the top slot, requiring highest public policy and planning attention. The secondary and indirect place, mainly by way of acting as an enabling state, assigned to the employment question and creation of jobs as a by-product of growth, accumulation, technological progress, macro economic balance and so on by almost every state or regime in the TWCs, such as India, is poles apart from the criticality of 'employment', i.e. productive and gainful participation in the economic activities of the nation, for obtaining the necessary wherewithal for living as social citizens. It seems reasonable to infer that it is owing to such disparate perspectives, that the problem of employment as an important component of development discourse, finds a secondary place in the neo-liberal perspective, that understates the extent and severity of the endemic and massive livelihood crisis seen in India in terms of the per capita expenditure data from the NSS. As highlighted by the report of the NCEUS (2008 and 2009), an overwhelmingly large part of the people of India are forced to live without any regular, adequate and visible means of satisfying the basic needs, that living creates or involves. This is clearly because both the mainstream market-centric economic activities and the economic and social activities and interventions by the neo-liberal state hardly privilege the needs, rights and aspirations of the people at the lower rungs of society, say, in terms of treating the state as the Employer of the Last Resort (ELR). Such a perspective can come to prevail only when the wider social perspective, in terms of social markets and democratic government, striving for real development, that puts an end to social exclusion, is adopted. Clearly, such a perspective is the polar opposite of the neo-liberal perspective that finds no place for the wider connotation of employment, as the major means for sustainable livelihood, as a universal right. The concept of development, with the growth of per capita national product, postulated by the mainstream economics of development, rather stubbornly in the face of its near universal rejection, introduces some democratic social normative content in it and inevitably makes universal livelihood right, an in-built component of development. As a corollary of such a comprehensive concept of development, a view has come to be advanced by some influential scholars, known for their objectivity, expertise and insights in the problems of the TWCs, to underline the close affinity between the problems of poverty, unemployment and inequalities, bedevilling the existence of the poor in these countries (J. Tinbergen, 1979, D. Seers, 1979). Actually, the recent practice of defining the problems of the poor countries, by means of and in terms of social exclusion of the masses, also leads one in the direction of visualising the close affinity between these three main problems, of what the mainstream economics of development also identifies as the main but largely distinct problems of these countries.

It takes but a little reflection, on the theoretical foundations and historical experience of neo-liberalism, to show that its agenda is consistent with widespread denial of livelihood rights and opportunities to a large part of the labour force (the real meaning and essence of what is generally called employment). Actually, matters go far worse from the employment angle as the neo-liberal practices have often caused endemic and recurring unemployment or sacrificed sizeable volume of employment on the altar of economic growth under the auspices of organised, large, generally corporate capital, both by its deepening and widening and extension of its sway over every aspect of the economy and society. The essential point of these neo-liberal employment theories is that increased employment in terms of the definition of employment for special purposes, that it has devised, is consistent with worsening inequalities, persistent hunger and malnutrition and unregulated and socially indifferent determination of investment and production decisions by the market operators! Growth, based on some perverse set of investment decisions, say, for example seen in most of the market economies, old or emerging, by reckless financial market speculation leading to financialisation and extreme volatility, as one of the most dynamic contributors to growth and corporate profits, tends to be paraded as freedom from crisis and recession, even though the army of retrenched workers, keeps on swelling. How the odyssey of India with neo-liberalisation and accelerated GDP growth, for the past two decades, has sacrificed enormous opportunities for generating really effective and decent employment, is what we are going to examine in this exercise. But the reality of what has happened, is so compelling that the Indian policy establishment has little hesitation in recognising that "the relatively higher rate of growth, achieved during the last decade or so is not seen to generate a sufficient volume of good quality employment" (11th Five Year Plan, p.63). However, it is not clear whether this outcome is considered a contingent, transient factor or something basic, long-term and substantive.

Put briefly, since the beginning of 1990s, the following can be observed as the main features of the emerging socio-economic landscape of India: unregulated markets and self-interest-driven pursuit of corporate goals, especially in the financial sector, absence of regular and sizeable markets for mass consumption goods (itself a function of a situation, in which the masses are not endowed with regular access to adequate purchasing power), powerful economic impact of a borderless economic world on the indigenous processes of resource allocation, investment decisions, technological choices, determination of the pattern of international trade, hyper growth of financialisation, growing influence of the cultural counterparts of the processes of neo-liberlisation and globalisation (in the form of putting premium on self-centred asocial existence and values of acquisitive hedonism, privileging symbols over substance, etc.). It can be seen that the above factors have combined together to help the Indian economy move on to a higher growth trajectory but have also at the same time and as a part of the same process, accelerated the marginalisation and multi-faceted exclusion of the resource-poor and voiceless masses (See for a lot of evidence from official sources, the reports of the GOI, NCEUS, 2009). It is the operation of these inherited and currently accentuated forces and processes that increasingly deny any critical agency function and rightful and rewarding participation to the poor masses; in fact, going so far as to deprive a huge majority of the minimum basics needed for survival.

It is these features of the neo-liberal path that can show how and why a negative correlation has come to operate between neo-liberalism on the one hand, and adequacy and security of employment (or the creation of sellers' market conditions in the labour market), on the other. It seems that it is in this context that as an after thought, as a posture and defensive strategy and as add-ons, borne of political, economic and some moralistic and public relations compulsions, various ostentatious programmes of 'inclusive growth', consistent with the basic nature and thrust of neo-liberalism are often announced by the Indian state. This kind of inclusive growth agenda may well be taken to underline the non-acceptance and incompatibility of universal livelihood adequacy and security with the neo-liberal creed, over a foreseeable length of time. In fact, as far as the organised big capital segment of the poor economies is concerned, its capacity to absorb any significant part of the huge labour force has been extremely weak; it is further weakened, by the periodic fluctuations it experiences, owing to its failure to generate adequate aggregate effective demand. Thus it may sound paradoxical that the economies based on generalised commodity production, have, in real life, failed to fully commoditise, as critical, an input, as labour. One can see how only less than 10 per cent of the Indian labour force has been lucky enough, to successfully find employment in the organised sector and that too, without any assurance of decent employment, involving a living wage and a measure of social security. It is well known that over 90 per cent of the Indian labour force has no option but to eke out their living, outside the organised labour market, often in arenas of small commodity production, by working on one's own account. This is also a factor that shows how inadequate livelihood opportunities derive from and contribute to India's notorious inequalities, in addition to intensifying chronic mass poverty and deprivation.

As a part of such neo-liberal inclusive growth, another device is often resorted to, to polish its credentials with respect to what is called the unemployment problem. As really effective sustainable livelihood opportunities fall woefully short of the required quantum, the people who are left high and dry are forced to devise of their own, various coping strategies for survival. In this process, they also make extensive use of the traditional occupations and also devise new ones. Quite a few of these make-do, decentralised, local level activities tend to cater to the needs and wants of the poor for low-priced goods and services which they cannot meet through the normal market and state-provisioned channels, owing to the exclusion caused by the highly concentrated, oligopolistic market processes. This is because the normal, unregulated and narrowly controlled market processes in a unilaterally created borderless world, under the patronage of a protective, facilitating and ideologically committed state, concentrate their resources on the production of high income goods with rather low employment-creating capabilities. Since most of the high income, highly capital, energy and import-intensive goods are not affordable by the poor masses, the inadequate supplies of mass consumption wage goods, constrains the process of productive absorption of the available labour force, at a fair and adequate wage rate, let alone with any sense of security. The exclusionary effects of lack of work opportunities cannot be reversed if increased employment is not accompanied by increased flow of goods and services, affordable by and appropriate to the needs and life style of the new entrants into the work force (Kabra, 2007, Indian Journal of Labour

Economics). Hence, there emerge a host of activities on the sidelines of the organised mainstream market processes, in which the excluded people find refuge for survival.

It is clear, we are referring to the celebrated and significant phenomenon of the informal or unorganised economy that forms a reckonable part of the economy of India and performs one of the key functions of the economy, that is, creation of relatively easily available avenues of livelihood and extended reproduction, generally at levels that fall short of a decent minimum but nonetheless, presently the only set of activities that discharge this task for an overwhelmingly large number of Indians. This essentially survival sector is the most significant source of livelihood and supply of many essential wage goods and services to the masses of poverty-stricken people. Indian official policy and planning establishment too acknowledges the significant contribution made by this part of the economy. Actually, many policies and programmes are specifically directed to cater to the needs of this non-formal segment. Ironically the Indian employment data shows the contribution of this sector, based largely on the failure of the mainline organised economy, also as a part of the growth of employment opportunities and implicitly attribute the credit for it to the neo-liberal growth policies. True, some of the employment in the informal economy does owe itself to the positive linkages and spread effects of the growth in the organised sector. But the quality of the work opportunities in the informal economy, with some honourable exceptions, (either made due to the inability of the organised economy to create space for the productive utilisation and inclusion or derived from the spread effects and linkages of the organised sector growth) remains far from satisfactory. Neither the level, amount, regularity of remuneration nor the conditions of work, prospects of survival and improvement of most of the informal work, are up to the standards that can satisfy the conditions required of decent work opportunities. The public policy support to the informal economy is also mainly token and grossly inadequate in terms of, both the needs of the informal sector as well as when compared to what is provided to the organised and corporate sectors. Such employment cannot have any long term future unless the whole economy is re-organised, sans excessive and dysfunctional concentration at the top, leading to the creation of a decentralised and equitable social economy.

Thus, what comes across, as either the employment performance of the neo-liberal regime or the targets for the purpose, have to be taken with a pinch of salt, as a part of them is only negatively related to the policy regime and only one part is related to the impulses, emanating from the growth of the organised segment. At best, it is a transitional attainment that provides the much needed immediate run support and succour, needed in an economy, that has no universal social security cover for the people who need it most.

There are a number of other features of the informal sector and the neo-liberal pro-big capital policies that make one question if there is any significant degree of utility of it on a long-term basis for generating viable and dependable means of livelihood for the excluded people as contrasted with enabling the excluded, to just about subsist. In this sector, generally wage rate is low and own-account workers get volatile remuneration. In one word, this sector is home to a large part of the 'working poor.' Often piece rate system of wages and contract supplies to the organised sector entities, based on work carried out at home, are factors that make for low level of uncertain incomes for informal workers. Hence, their capacity to save and invest or provide for a rainy day, are also limited. Its internal capacity for competitive and higher return yielding process or product innovations, is limited and uncertain. The fact that even the formal and corporate sectors often switch over to informal forms of hiring employees, in order to cut costs, signifies the low quality of this kind of work or employment.

Actually a major limitation, crippling the employment potential of the organised capital and corporate sectors, the chosen growth agents and leaders under the neo-liberal framework, is that market determined investment and production decisions are excessively influenced by the existing market demand, dominated by the magnetic pull of the demand of the high income groups of elites. Price signals have no capacity to send messages, regarding the enormous volume of unsatisfied needs of the socially excluded sections (notwithstanding the rhetoric of the massive demand at the bottom of the pyramid) who have little command over regular flows of purchasing power, to tilt the scale of the relative rates of return on invested capital. Nor are markets known for expanding their ambit, by incorporating or including those who are outside their ambit, owing to lack of regular and sufficient income and or productive assets or market-oriented skills that can find patrons among the xenophile well-to-do sections. Thus the relative rates of return from the mass consumption goods sector, remain low and unattractive. Actually even if the state pumps in some income by way of providing some relief to the excluded sections, the relative rates of return from this kind of production are unlikely to lead to creation of production capacities on any sizeable scale, let alone creation of secondary rounds of expansion for generating new employment opportunities. Lately, the tendency of the large foreign and domestic corporate capital to enter arenas that have conventionally remained more or less exclusive preserves of the small and decentralised sector of private capital, such as retail and placement services for personal and community services, for example, have further added to the shrinking space and low returns from the informal activities. Price signals have no capacity to send messages regarding the enormous volume of unsatisfied needs of the socially excluded sections. Hence the enormous market at the bottom of the pyramid remains an empty, non-realisable projection as long as the investment decisions are guided by the calculus of relative rates of return and their rates of growth, over time.

Given the pull of existing concentrated purchasing power, a certain measure of curbs on this source of demand is also an essential part of the genuine policies for employment creation but is simply inconsistent with the neo-liberal orthodoxy. In simple terms, increasing real effective employment, without a commensurate increase in the absolute quantity and relative proportion of wage goods, is a mirage. One can see that the neo-liberal inclusive growth agenda fails to appreciate these pre-conditions and hence are largely ineffective in making a dent, in the massive livelihood crisis faced by the majority of the people in India. It has also to be recognised that there are major political and power-based hurdles, that prevent the really effective employment approach, from seeing the light of day. While it is true that these hurdles are real and cannot be assumed away, at least in the short-run, the analysts and policy advisers, still have little justification for internalising these and suggesting only the things, that are considered by them, on unstated basis, as doable in the present political economic scenario. No, one must not allow the scientific and objective analysis from the point of view of the excluded masses, to be hijacked by the present establishment and its apologists.

At this stage, one may draw attention to a fatal flaw of neo-liberal policy packages, in relation to the objective of universalisation of the right to livelihood or at least a right to employment. The neo-liberal approach proceeds in terms of taking employment as an indirect function or a secondary effect of investment, production, trade, technology, location and such like decisions of the private entrepreneurs, provided their decisions are not interfered with, by legal and social regulations. It is rare indeed to find either any mention of the pattern of investment, production and growth, as having a bearing on the employment potential, unleashed by the neo-liberal processes or at times, it finds a ritual mention but is soon forgotten. Even when for the sake of completeness, the words like 'pattern of production', 'investment' and so on are mentioned along with the need to make it more broad-based, it seems that this is more for the form's sake than for actual substantive guidance (World Bank, 2010, p 7). One would hardly have any ground for disagreeing with a similar position, when it says that "reversal of the adverse employment related outcomes requires reversal of the pattern of economic growth" as seen in the recent past. (Idem, p.63, emphasis ours). But in the absence of policies to change the factors underlying the employment-hostile pattern of demand, production and distribution of income and wealth, some token action for ad hoc public work opportunities, cannot change the pattern in any employment-friendly direction. Actually the competitive urge for maintaining high rates of profitability, market valuation of assets and control over a growing part of the market are quite strong and pervasive. Hence the fundamentalist forces of market regard the freedom of the employers to be able to hire and fire, without state intervention, in the midst of buyers' market conditions as prevalent in India, a major pre-condition for these market forces to carry out their agency function. Expectedly in such a framework, the employment implications would remain an incidental outcome. In any case, even with the fulfilment of these pre-conditions, there is hardly any assurance that the process of employment generation would absorb the entire available labour force unless the wage rate is so flexible as to keep moving down until every one is hired. But hiring labour at a wage rate lower than the minimum essential for survival and reproduction, cannot be considered employment in the real sense of the term. Thus private entrepreneurs, enjoying the freedom to hire and fire, have little reason to exercise the right to hire to such an extent that they have to face a sellers' labour market condition. Clearly in an economy with a huge reserve army of labour, the scales remain tilted against the labouring masses, as the employers prefer a buyers' labour market.

Actually, the whole neo-liberal ideology is based on considering labour as a commodity at par with all the other inanimate goods and services and not as social beings, who as citizens of a democratic state, at par with the employers, are also the entities for whose needs, the economy is organised. Now many mainstream economists too have come to accept the essential social character of the labour market, as a social institution, whose character goes much beyond the market processes. Hence they discard the pure market approach to employment and labour. Insistence on full scale labour market flexibility cannot ensure that full employment, meeting the conditions of decent employment, can ever emerge. Actually, a purely economic labour market is nothing but a fiction. However, one comes across the phenomenon of massive unemployment of adult labour, co-existing with a great deal of hiring of child, indentured and coerced labour (things that in most countries fall outside the pale of legality and are considered socially and culturally repugnant). These phenomena suggest that factors such as extra-economic coercion, resort to unethical and illegal practices, use of political influence and power, weakness of collective bargaining and social movements on labour rights, excessively self-centred, pro-profit values and so on, to influence the labour market practices.

In view of what we have maintained so far, it is clear that the right to work or commitment to full employment or the right to livelihood and participation on fair and equitable terms in the entire gamut of socio-economic and cultural life of society, are mattes that are not in keeping with the declared and well-known position of the neo-liberal policy establishment. To them, inequalities whether inherited, existing and/or increasing over time, are normal market phenomena or outcome and cause little concern, or offer hardly any option of escape. Hence, massive and chronic unemployment do not matter to them, except the phenomenon of absolute poverty, that is believed to pose serious economic and social threats to the stability and sustainability of the neo-liberal dispensation. It is for some such reasons that mostly low quality informal and irregular employment or own account work with harsh working conditions, low productivity and low and uncertain rewards are also treated as employment by the neo-liberal establishment, just as informal and casual employment in the formal, organised sector is treated as employment, without any regard for the quality of employment or the appreciation of the marginalised labour force, in the same way as equal-rights enjoying co-citizens. Thus the claims regarding employment generation, whether actual or likely ones, by means of policy changes, in the countries following the neo-liberal policy path, must be interpreted carefully, as there is a lot of mix up of bananas with apples and so on, that is, simple survival-subsistence activities too are treated as employment.

What seems to emerge from the foregoing is that neo-liberalism is neither interested in nor capable of assuring full employment, or even a level of employment essential for full installed capacity utilisation, as long as it does not snowball into an overall downturn or recession. What we are treating as the litmus test of employment, that is, livelihood adequacy and security to everyone, irrespective of the level and rate of growth of the economy and its top echelons, does not sit well with the nature and perspective of the forces, supporting the neo-liberal development path. Furthermore, whatever little priority is forced by the socio-political and economic compulsions, to accept, is rarely carried out by means of direct interventions but is done by means of accelerating the rate of growth of the economy, supported occasionally by some short-run public works programmes for placing some amount of purchasing power in the hands of the excluded sections. Such largely flower pot schemes become acceptable, owing to their potential to increase demand in the home market and reduce the political costs of maintaining the facade of democracy.

The neo-liberal state, contrary to a popular myth, does not withdraw from the economic sphere. It basically changes the objectives of its economic interventions, in the direction of enabling the supposedly self-regulating market processes and forces, to facilitate the process of capital accumulation by the market players, in a borderless world. In this context, one also comes across policies that sacrifice employment generation, in order to accelerate growth and related processes and structures. Thus it can be said that on the one hand, the neo-liberal growth path may attempt to increase its role for employment generation but on the other, it would do so by claiming to combine these with the freedom of enterprise and markets.

II

Employment and livelihood scenario during the last two decades of Neo-liberalisation

Given the above critique and rejection of the neo-liberal concepts and measures of employment as also indicating the limited scope and space for a pro-employment thrust, we begin with an assessment of the ground level situation, regarding employment in India, during the period of full scale and open operation of the neo-liberal policy package. We repeat that we proceed to examine the issue, taking employment to mean livelihood adequacy and security by means of work, that, over time, results in output flows at least equal to the level of livelihood and define the employment objective as moving towards a seller's market condition in the labour market. This has to be counter-posed vis-a-vis the official Indian position based, as mentioned above, on a different conceptual and measurement system and at an operational level, it defines no time horizon, for ensuring employment to every one as a matter of right.

But when it comes to appraising employment performance for any given period, as far as the labour force and work force data are concerned, there does not seem to be any alternative to the NSSO data. Irregular or low-earnings employment can, of course, be inferred from the NSSO consumption data, supplemented by the data from the Economic census but for informal and formal employment data. That is how the income for financing consumption is obtained; some additional information is required. All the statistics, in the following, are obtained from various reports of the NCEUS and a World Bank study (cited above). Thanks to the work of the NCEUS, today both quantitatively and on the theoretical and policy planes, there is a lot more clarity on these questions than at any time in the past.

In the year 1993-94 and 2004-05, labour force was estimated at 345.15 million and 429.88 million respectively, with corresponding work force at 326.97 million and 401.13 million. Labour force is projected to be about 502 million in the year 2012. With annual addition to labour force, placed at about 12 million persons, the current level of labour force may roughly be about 480 million. It may be mentioned that fork force includes not only those engaged in regular gainful activity but also those who are engaged in gainful activity, occasionally. Clearly, inadequate income earning persons too are treated as employed. A separate category for low earnings employment, it seems, is required for a more nuanced appreciation of the overall employment scene. This is another indication that the official data on employment estimates, remain unconnected to the adequacy and security of access to the means of livelihood and reasonable productivity. A special feature of the labour market emerging in India presently, is that 60 per cent of the labour force is under 30 years of age, indicating that the additions to the labour force are going to be large. The difference between labour force and work force is taken to show open unemployment. Open unemployment, according to these data, increased from 18.18 million persons in 1993-94 to 28.75 million persons in 2004-05. Thus, in terms of the conventional measures, unemployment rate of about 8 per cent seems to plague the Indian economy. What is notable is that while labour force increased at the rate of 2.02 per cent per annum, the work force increased at a rate of 1.88 per cent and unemployment rate increased at over double the rate of growth of labour force and work force.

Another aspect of the employment scene is also of critical significance. Most of what has been called employment is in the informal sector (over 90 per cent) or what the NCEUS calls "informal work in the informal economy." In the sense in which we have chosen to treat employment, only "formal employment in the formal sector" can be treated as real and effective or full sense employment. This is important in so far as lately most of the new employment in the formal sector too has been informal. Let us just recall how informal workers have been defined: "those who do not have employment security, work security and social security" (NCEUS,2008, 11 and NCEUS, 2009, 12). It is clear that such 'workers' are prominent among those who are considered socially excluded sections of society.

Based on the subjective perception based concepts, measures and surveys, a concept of 'working poor' has evolved, that shows that despite working, or being a part of the work force, a large number of people remain poor in terms of getting wages below poverty line consumption expenditure. Recent estimates have put the number of working poor at around 105 million, that happens to be about a quarter of all workers (World Bank, 2010-11), and is well below any estimate of the number of poor. On the other hand is the fact that even the most conservative estimate of poverty numbers (based on a level of consumption expenditure that cannot find justification on any ground whatsoever, except the unwillingness of the establishment to be just and fair to the people) puts the number of poor at a multiple of 105 million (the latest estimate that seems to find favour in government circles puts the proportion of the poor at around 37 per cent of population of about 112 crore). Thus, a very large number of people who are considered a part of the work force are in fact, poor and greatly below the mean income of about Rupees Forty Thousand per annum, showing a disconnect between poverty elimination, inequalities and employment. This oddity occurs because, as suggested above, adequacy of the reward of work as income and productivity of work, in terms of output flows, have not been treated as essential requirements of meaningful employment, both from the micro and macro-social points of view. Or put another way, work force has been taken purely in a quantitative sense, without any regard for the qualitative aspects of work, in terms of what is called decent work. These facts put a serious question mark on the practice of restricting the rate of unemployment to 8 per cent or so and putting the number of working poor at 105 million and attempts to understand the question of employment, in terms of the three measures deployed by official agencies. (A well reasoned critique of these measures is available in the NCEUS, 2009, pp.7-8). These measures give exaggerated and misleading estimates of employment in so far as a large number of people who are considered employed, continue to suffer acute livelihood crisis and are denied opportunities, to make any contribution to social-economic activities and hence are forced to remain socially excluded .

In order to make sense of the employment situation in a meaningful sense, consistent with basic economic criteria and as befitting social citizens, one has to see what such officially declared employment means to the social existence of the people at the level of ground reality. One may again fall back upon the NCEUS (2009). It shows how " a large proportion of the Indian work force and the Indian population (more than three-quarter) continues to be "poor and vulnerable" (p.10). Though the proportion of population suffering from extreme poverty and living below the so-called official poverty line (approximately Rs.12 per day per capita consumption in 2004-05) came down significantly from 1993-94 onwards (though the decade, starting from 1993-94 saw deceleration of the growth of employment - KNK) they seem to have moved only marginally above the poverty line and about 77 per cent of them were stuck below the expenditure on an average of Rs 20/- per day per capita. We describe these people as Poor and Vulnerable, as against the remaining 23 per cent of Middle class and Higher Income groups." Even this level of average consumption is quite low compared to the World Bank poverty line (PL) of US $1.25 and is incapable of meeting even the basic minimum need of an individual. What is shocking is the hypocrisy involved in such a determination of the PL and keeping it unchanged (save adjustment for rising general price level) despite several fold increase in per capita real GDP and tall claims of following a policy of redistribution from growth by 'experts' who miss no occasion to add disproportionately, to their already sky-high, even obscene level of pay and perks.

What follows from the above is that the actual volume of employment that is reported in the official statistics does not indicate the number of persons who are able to meet at least their basic needs. After all, what is the meaning of employment if it is not able to provide even the minimum of basic human needs?

This is quite contrary to the rosy prospects of profusely generated employment opportunities that were put forward by those who introduced a major overhaul of the policy course (tendentiously described as 'reforms') towards free flow of entrepreneurial energies as disclosed and enlarged by the self-regulated global-scale market forces. Let us briefly see what has really happened to employment during the last two decades, even in terms of a grossly misplaced understanding of employment, with a built-in bias to under-report unemployment. Here is the conclusion reached by a recent study of employment issue in India by the World Bank (2010). It says that over the last two decades (1983- 1994 and 1994-2004) both for principal and subsidiary workers, employment growth was largely flat or slightly declining from 2.1 per cent in the first decade to 1 per cent in the second. It goes on to say that with higher growth post-2000, employment numbers increased but there has been a deceleration in the growth of wages and earnings, mainly for the workers in the middle group (p.1).

Similar findings have been arrived at by the NCEUS, 2009. It shows that despite higher growth rate, employment growth decelerated and then quality of employment deteriorated as 86 per cent of employment in 2004-05 was "informal employment in the informal sector." Furthermore, there has been informalisation of a large incremental part of the formal sector employment. And even more disturbingly, "the growth rate of wages of almost all categories of workers, including casual work which concerns the bottom layer of workers has declined during 1993-94-2004-05 characterised by economic reforms compared to the previous decade of 1983 to 1993-94. This is clearly a case of generalised slow down in the growth of wages, when the overall economy registered a higher growth in income during the second period as compared to the first (p.9). Thus it is clear that "the growth that has occurred has been unequal, concentrating its benefits among the top segments of the population (p.10)." This is what we consider as an essential part of the process and dynamics of the neo-liberal economic and social processes: growing inequalities and wider dispersal of economic opportunities in the form of giving gainful employment at fair remuneration, simply do not go together.

Actually the larger part of employment in the unorganised sector is a built-in ingredient, as a safety-valve, as a spontaneous survival device, adopted by the excluded people in the face of exclusionary growth and also a mechanism that facilitates hyper growth of profits and surpluses, garnered by the top corporates and other businesses. Such dysfunctional concentration was given additional momentum by the expanding frontiers of cronyism under the neo-liberal framework in India, that moved on to the neo-liberal band wagon with the legacy of a huge amassing of illegal and ill-gotten wealth and underground relationships among the top political, bureaucratic and corporate echelons that became the decisive influence on the political-administrative and business decision-making. In such a situation most people have to fend for themselves either on unfair terms, at the bottom of the modern market economy or outside it, without regard to legality or morality, by means of a number of traditional or improvised means and devices, without regard to legality or otherwise. It is on account of such factors that we consider it important to examine the socio-economic information about the informal and the underground economies, as a substantive factor for understanding the real quest of the people for obtaining the wherewithal for living. Often, the informal economy has been treated as the residual of the formal sector. It comprises a variety of self or group, created small and often sporadically operating means and devices or callings, even some revived from the traditional and declining or practically defunct activities. Such activities are basically a function of human ingenuity and the struggle for survival, when pushed to the wall.

Luckily, lately a substantial source of information has become available in the form of the reports of the Fifth Economic Census. At least the last three reports give fairly comparative data for the period 1990, 1998 and 2005. These reports give quite detailed information about various facets of the informal sector. Actually the number of enterprises with more than 10 workers is a tiny fraction of the total number of establishments (they ranged between 3.13 per cent in 1990 and 1.51 per cent in 2005, with the number of persons usually working in them, declining from 37.11 per cent in 1990 to 25.52 per cent in 2005). From these, it follows that the number of persons usually working in these establishments, increased from about 26.75 million in 1990 to nearly 55.73 million in 1998 and then to almost 74.70 million in 2005. It may be noted that these figures exclude establishments engaged in crop agriculture and plantations and hence do not represent the economy-wide situation. Thus, over a period of about one and a half decades, the number of workers in the establishments in the informal sector, multiplied almost three times (Economic Census, 2005, All India Report, 2008, Chapter V).

Compared to such employment by proxy, the real and effective employment is what one finds in the formal sector. We have two estimates of the people who can be considered employed in terms of the adequacy and security of livelihood. The Ministry of Labour, GOI, monitors employment situation in the country on the basis of a legally backed reporting system from all the units in the organised sector. It has been shown that it has many snags and is considered generally to have an under-reporting bias. On the other hand, we have the data from the Annual Survey of Industries (ASI) that obviously does not cover areas other than industries. The number of organised sector workers has to be seen in the context of the overall labour supply, as emerging from the workforce participation. During the period 1993-94 to 2004-05, workforce participation rate fluctuated between about 40 per cent to 42 per cent (India Year Book 2009, Manpower Profile, IAMR, Delhi, p.173). It may be noted that supply of labour slows down because workers become discouraged and drop out of the labour force, due to fewer employment opportunities (World Bank, 2010, op. cit., p.6). The NCEUS gives an overall profile of employment in India, over the latter part of the neo-liberal era.

The increase in employment from 396 million to 426 million is essentially cosmetic in so far as that it also includes the preponderant presence of informal workers, who depend on the informal sector, as the most important source of livelihood. It is these 'employed workers' who form an overwhelmingly large part of the work force. As suggested earlier, most of these make-do work avenues are more of an attempt by the excluded persons to survive, rather than to overcome exclusion and join the mainstream of the economy, particularly in view of the absence of any social security cover, for the victims of social exclusion who seek at least a toehold in the economy by means of various make-do activities. In many cases, the conventional work avenues too are weakening, mainly owing to the economic stress on and shrinking space for the lower rungs of society, owing to hitherto unseen concentration of the goodies at the top. These facts also show how the growth of informality dwarfs proper formal sector salaried employment and about 63 per cent of the non-agricultural workers are self-employed. Even the proportion of the salaried, in the non-agricultural sector is less than the proportion of the casual workers: 17 per cent former against 20 per cent latter. Even the formal sector now increasingly hires workers on informal terms as over these five years of high growth, one has seen but comparatively small increase in labour absorption by the formal sector, on formal terms.

The number of organised sector workers was 2.635 crore at the end of fiscal year 1990 and it continued to increase and reached the peak of 2.824 crore at end of fiscal year 1997. While public sector organised employment remains over twice the number absorbed by the private sector, the former underwent a decline in absolute terms, from the peak of 1997 in so far as almost 15 million fewer persons are now working in the public sector. This is a pointed indicator of rolling back of the state at least from the labour market and is related to declining levels of public investment from 36 per cent in 1993-94 to 28 per cent in 2004-05 and for the Tenth plan as a whole 22 per cent of the plan investment. Private organised sector employment peaked in 1998, though it was only half the level of the employment in the public sector. Private manufacturing employment shows more or less similar changes, peaking in 1997 (also confirmed in terms of the ASI data for the factory sector). The present level of private organised sector employment, after a brief interlude of episodic expansion, has come back to mid-1990s level. In view of the intense lobbying, currently carried on by the organised big capital, both Indian and foreign, for permission and facilitation to enter retail trade and displace the small unorganised trades, one may observe that private retail employment has crawled up at a very leisurely pace and the promised employment boom has not materialised, even though the organised big capital has entered retail trade in a big way. It may be noted that employment in the organised private sector increased in the initial response to the neo-liberal turn of the policies. It could not however, sustain itself beyond 1998. These policies seem to have evoked positive response from the investors initially, particularly the corporate investors, as newer opportunities, lower transactions and business start up costs and access to global resources, markets as also the psychological impact of installing a market-friendly regime, changed the business sentiment. Also given the declared intention to roll back the state, disinvestment of the public sector units and doing away with industrial and import licensing regimes, enthused the market. Share markets also boomed and the economic climate and the political regime have certainly turned pro-corporate and pro-foreign investment.

However, before long, the employment scene came in for a reversal of fortunes. A declining trend set in soon and actual employment fell to a level, a little below 2.73 crore and practically wiped out all the additions to employment that were witnessed, post-1991-92. The NCEUS shows that as a result of the early 1990s policy change, "Growth was thus not only expected to be higher but also pro-employment, raising incomes among workers in the labour-intensive sectors of the economy" (p.9), but the expectation has been belied. It would indeed be naive to give credit for informal employment to the high order marketisation and globalisation. This has to be understood in terms of the change in policy stance and commitments. The neo-liberal path has concentrated the agency function for growth in the narrow top end of the economy with all the possible partisan support, for those who are already well-off. This has forced out the main chunk of the resource-poor majority of the labour force, from the mainstream market economy, through the intensified exclusionary processes, causing growth, without much real and effective employment and shrinking space for the small and micro enterprises, particularly owing to de-reservation policy and permission to freely import the goods that were hitherto reserved for the small sector. Under such a situation, it is the people's economy, the informal economy, that really acquires major instrumental role by opening a small window of some modest opportunities, in terms of some avenues, for wresting the means for bare survival. It is the informal sector that acts as a partial and limited antidote to the increasingly oligopolistic and elitist content of growth. One can see that in the small segments left out by the big players, the people acquire the agency function by means of and in the form of informalisation. The neo-liberal path, however, is a path that extends and intensifies the main springs of social exclusion, as public policy and expenditure support and state generated and supported economic opportunities and resources are perversely distributed, in favour of the agencies occupying the top slots of the market economy, inevitably spawning disequalising, employment-hostile growth. The formal sector, as we would see in the next section, gets all the public policy and expenditure support, without enforcing any norms of reciprocity and social pay-off. Thus informalisation of the economy is reflected in the fact that the unorganised sector continues to contribute a larger part of the GDP (over 57 per cent in 2007-08, CMIE, National Income Statistics, July, 2009, 75). However, the difficulty lies in the other facet of the unorganised sector: its income generation level is too small compared to the disproportionately large number of people, whom it has to support.

A look at the profile of formal employment according to various broad sectors of the economy, shows that the public sector accounts for about two-thirds of the total employment (nearly 1.8 crore persons in 2007) compared to the private sector's under 0.93 crore persons in the corresponding year. More importantly, we have seen above that the growth of formal salaried employment in the private sector, became sluggish shortly after the pro-private sector change of the policy regime. It poses a serious question about the nature of growth, in general and industrial growth, in particular, under the liberalised-globalised framework of the economy and the policy regime. Similarly, the public sector manufacturing employment, after reaching the high of 18.52 lakh in 1991, moved to a declining phase with the onset of the neo-liberal path and reached a low of 10.87 lakh in 2007. What is interesting is that the fall in public sector manufacturing is accompanied by a rising level of employment in public sector mining and quarrying. The export boom of iron ore and other valuable minerals, needed for industrial growth and also to satisfy the appetite for such minerals by Indian capital, may perhaps account for it. The amount of displacement caused by the expansion of mining in the forest and tribal areas and the consequent, permanent loss of livelihood opportunities, by generations of the tribal people, does not seem to have mattered. The most notable feature of public sector employment, a target for long, of the accusation of over-staffing in direct public services, is a huge shedding of its workforce. A serious issue emerges from the above. While industrialisation consisting primarily of the manufacturing sector is considered the main means of growth, in India, the evolution and growth of this sector has been disturbingly inadequate, volatile and employment unfriendly. The near stagnant level of its share in GDP and employment structure around 15 per cent seems to argue a case for a thorough re-think of the issue.

It has been pointed out that agriculture still remains the mainstay of employment in India. However, the share of agriculture in employment saw a reduction from 65 per cent in the early 1980s to 55 per cent presently. However, there has occurred a steeper fall in the share of agriculture in

GDP to about 17 per cent. It is another facet of the continuing weak relationship between growth and employment that has engendered a number of critical imbalances and dysfunctional features in the Indian economy, including its structural retrogression. Even the fastest growing sector, that is, services, contributed next to nothing to additional employment in the organised sector; and even the relatively robust growth sectors like manufacturing and power generation etc. - the star performers of the organised sector - moved away from decent jobs, based on mutual contract between the employers and the employees. As an inevitable result of the largely negative performance on the employment front, wage share in the organised industrial sector, halved after the 1990s. Under these conditions, it is no surprise that the recession-like conditions knocked at the doors of the Indian economy, as seen in the manufacturing sector slowdown in early 2007, even before the ill winds from the US and the European economies reached our shores.

The deterioration in the quality of employment is reflected in the trends in wages. We can again fall back upon the succinct findings of the NCEUS (2009). It shows that "the growth rate of wages of almost all categories of workers, including casual work which concerned bottom layer of workers has declined during 1993-94 to 2004-05 characterised by economic reform compared to the previous decade of 1983 to 1993-94. This is clearly a case of generalised slow down in the growth of wages when the overall economy registered a higher growth in income during the second period compared to the first (p.9). In this context, an interesting observation has been made by the World Bank study (2010, 8). It says that unlike the formal manufacturing sector, the growth in value addition during the late 1990s, in informal manufacturing, was passed on to workers in the form of higher wages and more employment. If one were to contrast this finding of the World Bank with a proposition, advanced in the Eleventh Five Year Plan, one would be able to see the clear-cut ideological bias of the Indian planners. In order to make the pattern of growth, foster employment generation, the Plan suggests giving "encouragement to the corporate sector to move in to more labour-intensive sectors." As for the unorganised enterprises operating in the labour-intensive sectors, it has been suggested by the planners to "facilitate the expansion of employment and output (p.79)." Is the difference between "encouragement" for the corporate sector that has acted miserly in sharing the gains in value addition, in the form of either better wages or more employment, not sharp and loud when one comes across the planners' view to just "facilitate" the informal sector, that has generously shared its economic gains, in the form of higher wages and more employment. Is it an incidental factor or does it reflect something deep-rooted?

Overall, a few things stand out as major features of the employment scenario of the economy that have, by and large, escaped attention. As pointed out years ago in the Alternative Economic Survey, the process of short-run macroeconomic policy planning and important economic decisions in government seem to be arrived at, without regular, say, annual monitoring of the employment situation. Even when the employment data became available, generally on the basis of five-yearly national sample surveys, there seem to be little evidence that these data are used for giving employment the priority that it deserves. After all, these data clearly bring out the inability of GDP-centric approach, to deal with it as a by-product of growth. Perplexingly, we also see that the overall employment numbers used to show the performance of the economy, in this respect and also by way of targets, for future, make no clear distinction between apparent employment by own account activities and wage-based work in the informal economy and real employment, capable of ensuring adequacy and security of livelihood.

Another important fact, rarely noted all along the planning process is that on a long term view of about six decades or so, the phenomena of positive rate of growth of GDP and positive growth of the number of unemployed persons have been taking place concurrently. What it also shows is that, whether growth has been slow or fast, overall and in specific phases, it could not prevent the number of unemployed persons (particularly in the objective sense of extricating people, from the trap of low and uncertain livelihood) from increasing. Most often, the conventionally measured rate of change in employment, has been judged on the basis of its comparative slow down or acceleration vis-a-vis the experience during the immediately preceding or earlier periods. These measures do not place the number or rate of growth in the context of the total size of the backlog of unemployment plus the current addition to the number of job-seekers. Thus, it has often happened that while the employment growth rate is shown as rising, the actual volume of unemployment, that is the number of people who are in the queue, waiting for proper and decent employment opportunities, too is rising.

Similarly, the emphasis on the employment elasticity of output growth too seems to be misleading as a more direct and effective tool would be to proceed from employment to output and work on the basis of output elasticity of employment. It may incidentally be pointed out that this approach would surely privilege the question of an appropriate product-mix, emphasising the production of wage-goods and services for the low income groups, from the point of giving employment real content, douse the inflationary fires and make for more indigenous production at decentralised locations. At least this seems to be a relatively more effective approach, as indicated by the inference from the Okun's law that maintains that a one per cent reduction in unemployment, helps bring about three per cent increase in output.

Thus we may conclude that the employment situation in India has by and large remained unattended in a real and effective manner as distinguished from some cosmetic, discretionary income transfer schemes, often narrowly targeted to specific socio-economic groups or regions. Little wonder that the early 1990s' switch over to the neo-liberal path has only added to the neglect, enormity and complexity of the problem; all these exercises taken together have barely touched the fringe of the problem. Two factors can be cited to vouch for our position. One, as of now, the number of Indians facing acute livelihood crisis and pangs of exclusion exceed the number of people, who are supposed to have chosen to make a tryst with destiny in 1947. Two, not only is it that, a relatively low priority to employment as livelihood guarantee, compared to GDP growth, continues, despite its utter and demonstrated failure to generate adequate employment. However, many structures, processes and policies that worsen the employment challenge or sidetrack the real issues, remain intact. Take for example the case of the directionally and conceptually path-breaking but grossly mismanaged and misdirected (in overall design and at the implementation stage) step of National Rural Employment Guarantee

Programme. It is an example of going two steps forward and retracing three steps. Its declared purpose is compromised by keeping it restricted to one person per family, leaving out the urban economy and not adjusting the permitted wage rate according to the real purchasing power of money. The exclusion of the urban people may well be reflecting the greater political clout of the myopic and hide-bound corporate and organised sectors, who fear that as a result of such a guaranteed access to at least a bare minimum of subsistence, to the urban labour force, the organised sector employers might have to pay higher wages, compared to the rates paid under the guaranteed work scheme in urban India.

Thus, it is high time that the specifics and generalities of the present economic model and its interface with the current policy regime are examined to see whether it is possible to zero in on certain aspects that negatively impact the employment problem and identify some lines of decisive positive interventions.

III

Policies that failed the labouring masses and how to move towards real livelihood guarantee for everyone

It is not sufficient and particularly helpful just to point out, as we did at the outset, how neo-liberalism is unhelpful and even incompatible with assured and adequate livelihood for every one, over a reasonable period of time, that any generation can be expected to wait for. The examination of the employment scenario over this period in the preceding part confirms our initial hypothesis of low, indirect and incidental attention to the employment question under both embedded and openly embraced neo-liberalisation of India, since the beginning of development planning under its different phases. Neither the operation of the economy by itself nor with state interventions, that is overall macroeconomic policies combined with specific sector and problems related policies, including some measures specifically termed elements of employment policies, have come anywhere near making an identifiable dent in the enormity and severity of the endemic livelihood crises, confronting a huge mass of the Indian labour force. It may be recalled that the dramatic and drastic reversal of the character of the declared policies was attempted two decades ago, inter alia, with the hope and belief that the recharged growth engine would bring about, in its trail, desired positive impact on the employment front, even though a discreet silence was maintained on the time horizon, to be able to employ every one.

Of course, the Indian economy has not remained a sleeping giant during the post-independence era and before its neo-liberal restructuring. The strides it made, have led to a definite and many-sided, large, positive impact. Hitherto unseen levels of total investments and the enlarged scale of activities did provide a lot of new entrants to the labour force, after equipping many of them with fairly high quality skills and capabilities, a secure place under the sun. However, the trouble is that those who had to miss jumping on to the growth bandwagon are too uncomfortably numerous, compared to those who did. The lack of such capabilities among those who could not make it, is basically for no fault of theirs, but owing to a set of perverted priorities and equally misdirected policies. An alternative past was possible just as an alternative future is awaiting the left out people if we are farsighted and have enough social commitment and strength, to struggle till we succeed to change the course.

One may recall some of the major employment policies that have been operated from time to time, especially after the supply-side neo-liberal policies became the main direction, form and arenas of state intervention. These are: some budget-supported public works programmes, lately supplemented by a demand-driven income supplementation programme for the rural families, some banks and other financial institutions' supported, micro-level productive asset-creation programmes along with certain measures to improve the supply side capabilities and information and placement channels, in order to equip the labour force and help it find and retain employment, including some laws to protect and promote the interests of the workers, vis-a-vis the stronger bargaining power of the large corporate employers. The need for such protective steps for the labour force is apparent from the ground level fact that the corporate sector is not too favourably inclined to give employment its due role. Is it not reflected in the fact that despite enjoying internationally, the comparative advantage of rather low rates of wages and operating in a capital-scarce economy (though lately the investment rate has climbed up to over one third of the

GDP), the corporate sector is spending as low as 8 per cent of the total cost of production, by way of its wage bill? Moreover, it is true that poor and ineffective enforcement of the provisions of the laws meant to protect labour's statutory rights, does cost the employers something for buying up political and administrative support. But is it not their own enlightened choice? How can any one then blame the labour protect laws for abysmally poor employment generation? Most of these measures are restricted to the formal sector. So much so, that a proposed law for somewhat similar ends, for the unorganised labour in rural areas and agricultural work force, has not been able to enter the statute book.

Neither growth acceleration, nor specific policies for throwing open the Indian economy along with rolling out a red carpet for foreign capital, seem to have made them inclined towards industries, technologies, product-mix, locations and so on, that absorb a reckonable part of the labour force and satisfy the litmus test of bringing about a net reduction in the severity of unemployment. Both the acts of commission and omission of the 'freed, lubricated and pampered organised big capital' have turned out to be grossly inadequate to make a difference to the unemployment problem and hence to the ordinary Indian.

We may allude to some specific policy arenas, particularly fiscal and monetary policies. Under the self-imposed 'fiscal discipline', public investment growth remained artificially restricted, according to some pre-determined quantitative limits, bearing little relation to the needs and resource generation capability of the real and financial economies. The fixation over the size of the fiscal deficit owes itself to the presumed crowding out effects of it and its adverse effect on the expansion plans of the corporate sector as also the cost of funds. This bias facilitates diversion of funds to the corporate and organised sectors whose poor employment contribution is a major highlight of the neo-liberal era. Then, huge amounts of tax revenue is being foregone year after year, in favour of the rich tax payers and big corporate entities; a virtual income transfer of over Rs.5 lakh crore out of a total budget of a little over Rs.11 lakh crore, for the year 2010-11 which is over twelve times the budget provided for the guaranteed 'employment' programme, meant for about 70 per cent of all the Indian families, living in rural areas! The meagre allocations for such public works programmes and starving the basic rural and social infrastructure of public investment support (the reason advanced for resorting to public-private partnership) kills their potential direct and indirect employment contribution. Given the dismal employment record of the organised private sector, of course including its largest component, the private corporate sector, whether in the manufacturing or the over-blown services sector, forgoing of such gigantic amounts is surely the unkindest cut in so far as employment generation is concerned.

Many policies and basic elements of the approach to development, such as the high priority assigned to mimetic pattern of industrialisation and associated pattern of urbanisation, consumption, energy use, infrastructure facilities on the one hand and neglect of the rural economy, agriculture and non-farm rural activities that India opted for, on the other, made output and employment poorly co-related. The former set of choices tended to increase the weight of the high income goods (quite a few of them are classified in the Indian official statistics as part of durable consumer goods) in the product-mix adopted by the expanding manufacturing sector with the consequent neglect or rather declining weight of the wage-goods sub-sector. This is not the kind of structural change that is conducive to creation of effective employment opportunities, in a stable macroeconomic environment. With the structural changes in favour of the services sector, liberal opening up of the economy, leading to an unprecedented import boom, extremely congenial policy environment given to the corporate sector that increased the share of surpluses vis-a-vis employees compensation, along with the impact of the on-going process of increasing inequalities and absence of domestic needs based innovations, gaining in prominence (despite over 100 per cent rebate on the R&D expenditure for tax purposes) the 1991 policy shock therapy too, have been responsible for the intensification of the livelihood crisis of the masses. Continuing inflation at varying speeds, all along the period, also eroded people's purchasing power, redistributed incomes in favour of the business firms and weakened the demand pull, towards labour - intensive activitties.

The simple point is : it is such public policies that exacerbate the inherent tendency of the private capital-led market economy (patronised by the neo-liberal dispensation as the leaders of the growth process) that make the domestic market narrow and even limits the scope for growth and employment creation by the small and micro enterprises, in the informal economy from reaching viability and sustained growth. The reservation policy for the micro and small enterprises and exposing them to grossly unequal import competition too, tended to reduce the capabilities of an employment-friendly sector. Take another fiscal monstrosity in so far as employment is concerned. The depreciation rate permitted by Indian tax laws is 25 per cent for machinery and equipment, compared to 10 per cent permitted in the OECD countries (World Bank, 2010, p.9). If capital intensity is encouraged by such abnormal policy measures, making a massive direct contribution to corporate profits and excessive use of capital, how would their employment record show a positive social thrust in the form of choice of labour-intensive methods of production? With such low contribution to employment and the increasing practice to go in for informal mode of employment, adopted in recent years by the private companies, any encouragement to them by means of public policies, is a direct contribution to growing unemployment.

The corporate lobbyists and the neo-liberal high priests, sitting in the government, complain of inflexible labour laws as holding back employment generation, but they never point to the disaster that has been caused by the depreciation provisions, low duty paying import of capital goods from the rich countries, with their well-known capital-intensity bias. It is futile to expect the corporate sector-led growth to become employment enhancing growth. It is worth noting that while the 11th Plan 'targets' mention that some 30 million jobs are expected to be created, owing to normal growth buoyancy, about 20 million jobs are expected to be the outcome of "selective innovative programmes and policies, leading to a changed pattern of growth" (p. 67. end note of Table 4.4). One does not find any mention of policies that can lead to a changed pattern of growth, that remains dominated by the corporate sector as is clear from the fact that during the last few years, its share in GDP has increased from 19 per cent to 23 per cent. The share in GDP of the corporate sector, that barely accounts for about 2 per cent of the total work force, is more than the share of agriculture that is the source of livelihood for about half the work force. It is inherent in the market processes that unless counteracted by powerful and pointed policy action, such initial imbalances tend to become self-reinforcing over time. In any case, with our skewed distribution of income and for want of specific fiscal and other measures to encourage greater equity and investment in high labour intensive wage goods sector, really meaningful employment growth has hardly any positive prospects.

Things have really gone from bad to worse with the bountiful fiscal sops and transfer of virtually looted land of the poor farmers and tribals to the SEZs, sponsored by the new Maharajas, who would lord over hundreds of kilometers of empires, over which many of the laws of the land would not apply. This aspect has been criticised by the NCEUS as well. It has said, "The informal sector enterprises face higher constraints on growth due to lack of access to credit, technology, marketing, skills, and also incentives. Various reports, surveys and studies, have brought this up, time and again. Despite such a long standing and perceived absence of a 'level playing field' for the micro as well as small enterprises, that are outside the definition of informal sector enterprises, policy attention largely catered to the creation of 'special playing field' for example in the formation of Special Economic Zones (and greater access to domestic and external institutional credit) for large corporate entities, further undermining the capacity of the micro and small enterprises to provide productive employment to the growing labour force" (2009, pp. 9-10). Actually one is yet to come across any evidence that rupee for rupee, the incentives and bonanza given to the big capital on the platter, by means of the SEZs' like arrangements, have produced outcomes comparable with much smaller support given to the village and small and micro enterprises!

We cannot take up all the policies and the wrong these policies have done to the millions engaged, in so far, a fruitless waiting for a decent job, but must point out how the policy of import liberalistion has turned out to be one of the biggest disasters in the form of silent de-industrialisation. It is clear that such a fate of industries imposes disastrous effect on maintaining the level of domestic employment, let alone the creation of additional employment creation. We call it silent because the policy establishment has blissfully turned a blind eye to it. True, our manufactured goods exports too have been increasing, but compared to the lead, stolen by the manufactured imports over domestic production, the contribution of exports is small. Moreover, the exports growth costs the public, a tidy sum in the form of the fiscal bounties, showered on the exporters year after year, on their total exports, rather than on the incremental exports. On the contrary, the import boom has imposed a heavy cost on the public exchequer because it has been encouraged by steady reduction of the import duties from the average of about 21.88 in 1999-2000 to 7.4 per cent in 2008-09 (Economic Survey, 2009-10, p.172). It is clear that the import boom can rightly be attributed to the policy of opening up and joining the WTO, in order to integrate the Indian economy with the economies of the rich G-7 countries. We need not go into the question of the boom in IT related services. Its main contribution is in terms of foreign exchange earnings and its employment contribution is only around six lakh workers. Among other factors that keep employment growth limited, is the low interest rate regime that tilts the balance towards high capital intensity, especially in view of the relatively larger market for high income goods, in view of intense inequalities of income.

Such anti-labour absorption thrust of the export and import policies (particularly to removal of quantitative restrictions on imports, bringing down average duty level on our imports vis-a-vis excise duties, entering into free trade agreements with a number of countries and groups of countries, as also low level of public investment in agriculture and allied activities, irrigation and land improvement, forestry, rural infrastructure and micro, small and village industries, heavy reliance on imported technology, virtual disappearance of the question of appropriate technology from the policy discourse, entry of big organised capital into retail trade to queer the pitch for the small and peripatetic traders, are among the factors that are inimical to employment generation. The basic fact, more or less common to all the policies and areas of intervention, is that there is hardly any evidence of giving a sharp and clear attention to the employment effects, let alone the question of overriding prominence to employment impact of the measures.

An example of how employment generation has remained a non-issue and even destruction of existing means of livelihood involved in some investment and 'development' projects, does not seem to have mattered to the policies, derived from growth. Market fundamentalist policies can be seen in the large scale acquisition of land for purposes of mining, mega industrial projects, setting up airports, power projects, setting up Special Economic Zones and even for setting up universities, by some big private companies (such as the notorious case of Vedanta in the coastal areas of Orissa) that is actually, a thinly veiled exercise to grab land for commercial purposes. Thus, it seems various investment projects for growth and modernisation have become freshly energised engines for social exclusion in so far as they displace many times more people than they incorporate in these high income activities. The loss of employment and livelihood, consequent on land acquisition on the basis of coercive, non-market, iniquitous terms and processes and criteria and by ruthlessly crushing the victims' protests, have to be treated as some kind of internal restructuring that sacrifices millions of citizens for the sake of the profits of a few and an employment-less pattern of globalised industrialisation. The tribal and forest dwellers in the Eastern and Central States of the country have particularly been harshly exposed to such losses of their small means of livelihood, without any positive and meaningful rehabilitation measures. In short, while the specific anti-employment policy actions have been aplenty, measures that give relatively high priority to provide secure means of livelihood to the deprived sections of society, have been few and far between.

The crux of the examination of the approach to and performance regarding employment is to be seen in the apparently technical approach of dealing with the issue, in terms of and by means of working for acceleration of the rate of growth and estimating the employment impact in terms of the employment elasticity of growth, without any signs of activism to enhance it. On the basis of both empirical evidence and powerful and irrefutable critiques, many scholars and authoritative reports and studies have exposed the inevitably negative, poverty and inequalities enhancing character and anti-mass livelihood and ecologically destructive results of attempting to understand and foster development in general and employment in particular terms of the GDP of a country. Neither as an indicator, nor as an objective and even as a policy instrument can development and employment policy formulation and interventions in terms of per capita national product, have been positively useful on the criteria of net additions to employment, reduced poverty, enhanced equity, better ecological balance and so on. This is not to deny the usefulness of GDP, per capita, as one among several ex-post indicators of the level of economic activities that are organised on the basis of exchange, through several market processes. The point is: even economic activities have dimensions far beyond the capacity of GDP to capture and surely development is too serious and wide an issue to be comprehended, simply in economic terms. Despite the general validity and near universal acceptance of the misleading and incomplete nature of the guidance provided by the GDP-based measures and occasional statements by the Indian authorities too, to bring in the pattern of GDP as a relevant factor, it seems to be an example of unshakable commitment of the present Indian policy establishment, that its world view does not extend beyond GDP.

Lately, there seems to be emerging, a high degree of shared understanding on the issue of the futility and counter-productive nature of the using of per capita GDP growth, as the summom bonum. Many alternative approaches tend to provide a comprehensive concept of development and related policies. Most of them accord a high priority to employment for every one. Actually, some of them establish universal livelihood adequacy and security as very intimately related aspects of poverty and inequalities and thus an integral part of the content of development, that involves a very high priority for swift and decisive movement towards universal, adequate and assured livelihood that improves in an equitable and eco-friendly manner over time, keeping in line with diverse cultures in different parts of the world (See ECLAC report). Such a situation would, of course, be reflected in a high and reasonably rising level of per capita national product. But there is no reason to believe that high and rising per capita income that does not consciously change its pattern and composition and shares the agency function widely among various sections of society, can be considered in a normatively acceptable sense, as a developing society that is moving towards a higher stage of development. The point worth noting is that in the alternative approaches, GDP is consistently and inevitably associated with its pattern that reflects its higher use-value and broader social goals dimensions rather than a fixation with its exchange value dimension alone, that is, without exclusive concern with the sheer

WAGES OF ASYMMETRICAL GLOBALISATION --- THE GREAT RECESSION, 2007 AND CONTINUING

A not-too-creditable level of performance on the livelihood issue, even in terms of the apologetic concepts and measures, used by the Indian official statistical system was further worsened, under the adverse impact of the global economic and financial crisis, that began shortly after the beginning of the 11th plan (Satyaki Roy, 2009, 72-76, and Ministry of Labour, Labour Bureau, 2008). As far as the 11th Plan goes, the global crisis, its timing, magnitude, spread, intensity, duration and impact on India were as unknown to the Indian planners as to any one else, more particularly to those who naively announced the end of the era of business cycles, in the highly industrialised countries.

Many estimates have been made of the job-loss caused under the impact of the global crisis, mainly in the export industries and to an extent, in the manufacturing sector, as a result of the direct and indirect effects. Initially, the Labour Bureau came out with the estimate, showing that about half a million jobs were lost during October-December, 2008, causing a 3.4 per cent loss in earnings. The most affected sectors were gems and jewellery, transport and automobiles, where employment declined by 8.58 per cent, 4.03 per cent and 2.42 per cent respectively, during this period. Textiles sector too lost jobs. Further information shows that during the period October 2008 - January 2009, the job loss was put at around 5.09 lakh. (Satyaki Roy, 2009, p.73).

It may be noted that as a part of the packages that were introduced in order to stimulate the economy, (involving a cost and transfers directly or indirectly of about Rs. 4 lakh crore) its employment effect remains indirect, uncertain and inadequate, compared to the loss of jobs that has come about. One fails to see any direct programme of either re-employing the retrenched workers or linking the support to the companies, to adherence of a condition to not remove any one from the rolls. As usual, only indirect support to employment, by supporting the companies, to preserve the market demand and maintain their capacity use and their bottom line, were introduced.

quantitative size, irrespective of the qualitative and social choice-based dimensions. The real meaning of these deeply rooted positions can be appreciated in terms of a very straight forward and clear statement by the NCEUS: "In an unequal society like India, a general policy of growth and employment would create winners and losers; some industries would prosper while others would be left behind; some workers may face better prospects while others remain unemployed or underemployed. Growth is never equally shared in an unequal society, not much trickles down in real life, i.e. when it does, it is at a snail's pace ... Growth through investment incentives inter alia increases capital's share of national income as well as wage differential between organised and unorgaised labour, i.e. between formal and informal work. Such accentuation of inequality can only be precluded if the unemployed and the working poor are targeted directly through public works programmes, with the state acting as employer of the last resort (ELR)" (2009, 22).

What has been argued above, clearly suggests that the persistence in the intensified unequal India, of the neo-liberal era, with the GDP-centric indirect, uncertain, inadequate and inequalities-fostering approach is basically anti-employment, especially owing to the dynamic interactions of various kinds in several socio-economic and political spheres that it would spawn over a longer run. This has been confirmed by the experience of India over the last two decades. The attempt to persist with more of the same and do nothing about changing the pattern of growth in an employment-friendly direction and propagate false promises of inclusive growth, by some token welfare and relief measures, while simultaneously strengthening the well-to-do section's command over and voice in the economy, polity, society and culture is something the country has been witnessing, for decades now.

References

Government of India, Ministry of Statistics and Programme

Implementation, Central Statistical Organisation, 2005, Economic Census, India, All India Report, New Delhi.

National Commission for Enterprises in the Unorganised Sector (NCEUS), Government of India, 2008, Report on conditions of work and promotion of livelihoods in the Unorganised Sector, New Delhi.

NCEUS, (2009), The Challenge of Employment in India: An Informal Economy Perspective, Volume I - Main Report, April, New Delhi.

Planning Commission, GOI, 2007- 2008, Eleventh Five Year Plan, Volume I, Inclusive Growth, New Delhi.

_____,(??) Mid-term Appraisal of 9th Five Year Plan, 2002-2007, June 2005, New Delhi.

_____,(??) Mid term Appraisal of Ninth Five Year Plan 1997-2002, NewDelhi.

National Social Watch, 2009, Citizens' Report on Governance and Development, 2008-2009, Daanish Books, New Delhi.

Kabra, Kamal Nayan (1993), 'Political Employment Planning in India', *The Indian Journal of Labour Economics*, October-December, 36 (4).

Alternative Survey Group, Indian Political Economy Association, 2009, 'Global Economic Crisis: A people's Perspective: Fiasco of Neo-liberalism', Daanish Books, New Delhi.

Roy, Satyaki (2009), 'Losers are once again who lost in the past', Alternative Survey Group, op.cit.

Mazumdar, Surjit (2009), 'The Global Economic Crisis and its Impact on Demand Conditions in India', Alternative Survey Group, op.cit.

Government of India, Ministry of Labour and Employment, Labour Bureau, 2009, Chandigarh.

Kabra, Kamal Nayan (2007), "Wage-goods, Universal Livelihood Security and Development Policy", *Indian Journal of Labour Economics*.

Seers, D. (1979), 'The Meaning of Development' in D. Lehmann (ed.)

"Development Theory: Four Critical Studies", Frank Cass, London.

The Economist (2009), The Job Crisis, March 14th.

World Bank (2010), 'India's Employment Challenge: Creating Jobs, Helping Workers by Poverty Reduction and Economic Management', Oxford University Press, New Delhi.

Centre for Budget and Governance Accountability (2010), 'How Inclusive is the Eleventh Five Year Plan: People's Mid-Term Appraisal'.

P.L.Gautam, C. Thomson Jacob,
G. Venkataramani, Y. Singh

Biodiversity and Indian Economy

India is one of the major leapfrogging economies of the world and it has demonstrated its economic resilience in the wake of the global economic debacle. It quickly recovered from the downslide and has shown positive signs of becoming an economic super-power by 2020. Though, the growth rate in the agricultural sector, which pulled down India's average annual growth rate in the last few years, has led to some serious concerns, it has been predicted that the "future belongs to nations who have grains and not guns,"[1] and India is well poised to fit that vision. The Indian economy may join that of China, in surpassing the size of the U.S. economy by 2050, to become a motor of global growth, according to a new forecast by Goldman Sachs, the investment bank. The United States is currently the world's largest economy. Goldman forecasts that the Chinese economy will pass that of the United States by 2035, while India will do the same about a decade later. India has moved onto a much faster growth trajectory than had previously been expected, fuelled by strong and steady productivity gains in its legions of new factories and service sector. The rise of India will lead to increasing global competition for resources and more pressure on the environment.[2]

The rich biodiversity endowments of India have the potential of turning into the core strength of Indian economy. It will form a strong foundation for sustainable development in the present day context of climate change and global warming. It has been emphasised that India, with a rich heritage in conserving biological resources, is faced with a major challenge of preserving the biological wealth and it should be tackled with a missionary

---

[1] "Civil Society", July 2010, pp. 6-8
[2] Anand, Giridharadas (2007), 'India projected to join China in surpassing size of the U.S. economy by 2050', International Herald Tribune.

zeal, especially by actively involving the youth, to whom the future belongs.[3] Biodiversity offers one of the widest spectrums of livelihood, goods and services and business opportunities. The Indian economy, heavily depends on export of material of biological origin, be it agricultural produce, forestry, non-timber produces, fisheries, products of animal husbandry, carbon sequestration, bio-prospecting, ecotourism, bio-fuel, natural beverages or textile fabrics.[4] The biodiversity is commercially utilised for making drugs, industrial enzymes, food flavours, fragrance, cosmetics, emulsifiers, oleoresins, colours, extracts and genes used for improving crops and livestock, through genetic intervention.[5]

Ecosystem Services of Biodiversity

A healthy biodiversity provides a number of ecosystem services, such as protection of water resources, soils formation and protection, nutrient storage and recycling, pollution breakdown and absorption, contribution to climate stability, maintenance of ecosystems and recovery from unpredictable events. The activities of microbial and animal species - including bacteria, algae, fungi, mites, millipedes and worms condition soils, break down organic matter, and release essential nutrients to plants. These processes play a key role in the cycling of such crucial elements as nitrogen, carbon and phosphorous between the living and non-living parts of the biosphere. Wetland ecosystems absorb and recycle essential nutrients, treat sewage, and cleanse wastes. In estuaries, mollusks remove nutrients from the water, helping to prevent nutrient over-enrichment and its attendant problems, such as eutrophication, arising from fertilizer run-off.

Trees and forest soils purify water as it flows through forest ecosystems. In preventing soils from being washed away, forests also prevent the harmful siltation of rivers and reservoirs that may arise from erosion and landslides. Around 99 per cent of potential crop pests are controlled by a variety of other organisms, including insects, birds and fungi. Many industrial wastes, including detergents, oils, acids and paper are also detoxified and

[3] Abdul Kalam, APJ (2010), Make biodiversity core strength of India's economy, newkerala.com.
[4] Compendium of Biological Diversity Act 2002, Rules 2004 & Notifications, 2010. Published by the National Biodiversity Authority, Chennai, India.
[5] Swaminathan, M. S. (2010), "Biodiversity, Development, Livelihoods", published in The Hindu.

decomposed by the activities of living things. Many flowering plants rely on the activities of various animal species - bees, butterflies, bats, birds etc. to help them reproduce through the transportation of pollen. More than one-third of humanity's food crops depend on this process of natural pollination. Many animal species perform an additional function in plant reproduction through the dispersal of seeds. Plant tissues and other organic materials within land and ocean ecosystems, act as repositories of carbon, helping to slow the build-up of atmospheric carbon dioxide, and thus contributing to climate stabilisation. Also, these provide food, medicinal resources and pharmaceutical drugs, wood products, ornamental plants, breeding stocks, population reservoirs, future resources, diversity in genes, species and ecosystems.[6]

Economic Valuation of Biodiversity

A wide range of industrial materials are derived directly from biological resources. These include building materials, fibers, dyes, resins, rubber and oil. In addition, biodiversity and the ecosystem goods and services provide a healthy economic system. In order to catch the attention of policy-makers and to support the conservation of biodiversity, environmental economists have described a number of values of biodiversity. At the level of individual products, genetic resources and their derivatives fetch prices that range from just a few cents to tens of millions of dollars per kg, and often command prices far higher than standard indicators of value such as gold (Table 1).[7]

Thus, clippings from the yew tree fetch some $ 0.75 per kg, but the anti-cancer drug taxol, which is made from these clippings, costs $12 millions per kg. Illegal trade in a breeding pair of the highly endangered Lear's Macaw can fetch $260,000 (Burrel, 1998) and tiger bones for traditional Chinese medicine are worth $3,000 per kg (Crawford Allen, 1999). These prices are one factor which may contribute to the decline of these species, without a raft of properly enforced, legal and policy measures.

---

[6] Background Information on the International Conference on Biodiversity in relation to Food and Human Security in a warming planet held from February 15 to 17, 2010 at the M. S. Swaminathan Research Foundation, Chennai, India.

[7] Kate, Kerry Ten & Laird, Sarah A. (1999), "The Commercial Use of Biodiversity- Access to Genetic Resources and Benefit-sharing", Earth Scan Publications Ltd., London, UK.

Table 1- Prices for Selected Genetic Resources and Derivatives

Commodity (in italics if not derived from genetic resources)	Retail price per kg or litre (in $)
Human growth hormone	20,000,000
Taxotere/docetaxol	12,000,000
Vincristine sulphate	11,900,000
Cocaine	150,000
Camptothecin	85,000
Lear's Macaw	24,000
Gold	10,000
Dry bear gall bladders	7,000
HIV protease inhibitor	5,000
Saffron	6,500
Tiger bones	3,000
Italian truffle	650
Shark fin (personal care)	550
Coffee	10
Cotton	1.5
Petrol	1.0

Source: Kerry Kate and Sarah, 1999

In the recent report, The Economics of Ecosystems and Biodiversity (TEEB) for National and International Policy makers 2009 provided the following example of sectors, dependent on genetic resources (Table 2).[7]

Economic Importance of Biodiversity
Agro-Biodiversity

Agriculture is both a source of basic sustenance -food (nutrients and calories) for people, and of raw materials for industries. Agriculture is central to the livelihood of the rural poor and with over a billion workers worldwide, it is the largest economic sector, in terms of employment. It is also the sector where the majority of the world's poor and extremely poor is concentrated. Agriculture is fundamentally dependent on biodiversity and on ecosystem services. Species of crops and livestock and their genetic diversity are the basis of agriculture. Crop genetic diversity provides the materials for human societies to adapt to climate change. In India, agriculture remains one of the dominant drivers and mainstay of economic growth. India has over 800 crop species and 320 wild relatives: millets (51); legumes (31); fruits (109); spices and condiments (27); vegetables (54); fiber crops 924); oil

Table 2- Sectors depending on Genetic Resources

Pharmaceutical	$ 640 bn. (2006)	25-50% derived from genetic resources
genetic resources	$ 70 bn. (2006) from public companies alone	Many products derived from genetic resources (enzymes,microorganisms)
Agricultural seeds	$ 30 bn. (2006)	All derived from genetic resources
Personal care, Botanical and Food & Beverage industries	$ 22 bn. (2006) for herbal supplements $ 12 bn. (2006) for personal care $ 31 bn. (2006) for food products	Some products derived from genetic resources represent 'natural' component of the market

Source: Kerry Kate and Sarah, 1999

seeds, tea, coffee, tobacco and sugarcane (12); and medicinal plants (3,000). About 80 per cent of our food supply comes from just 20 kinds of plants; however, humans use at least 40,000 species of plants and animals a day. Many people around the world, depend on these species for their food, shelter, and clothing. There is untapped potential for increasing the range of food products suitable for human consumption, provided that the present high extinction rate can be stopped. Crop diversity is also necessary to help the system recover when the dominant crop type is attacked by a pest. In history, diseases have caused havoc to human societies such as:

- The Irish potato blight of 1846, which was a major factor in the deaths of a million people and migration of another million, was the result of planting only two potato varieties, both of which were vulnerable.

- When rice grassy stunt virus struck rice fields from Indonesia to India in the 1970s, 6273 varieties were tested for resistance. One- an Indian variety was found to be resistant, known to science, only since 1966. This variety provided the source of resistance.

- Coffee rust attacked coffee plantations in Sri Lanka, Brazil, and Central America in 1970. A resistant variety was found in Ethiopia.

- Monoculture, the lack of biodiversity, was a contributing factor to several agricultural disasters in history such as the European wine industry collapsed in the late 1800s, and the US Southern Corn Leaf Blight epidemic of 1970.

Higher biodiversity also controls the spread of certain diseases as pathogens need to adapt to infect different species.[8]

Livestock Genetic Diversity

India, endowed with varied forms of animal genetic resources, is traditionally considered as an important rearing centre for domesticated animals. India has vast resources of livestock (485 millions) and poultry (489 millions), which play a vital role in rural livelihood security. In terms of population, India ranks first in buffaloes, second in cattle and goats, third in sheep, fourth in ducks, fifth in chicken and sixth in camels in the world. The genetic resources of farm animals in India are represented by a broad spectrum of native breeds of cattle, buffalo, goat, sheep, swine, equine, camel and poultry. There are around 140 listed breeds of livestock and poultry in India, with 30 breeds of cattle, 10 of buffalo, 42 of sheep, 20 of goat, 3 of pig, 6 of horse and pony, 8 of camel and 18 of poultry. Besides, there are breeds of yak, mithun, ducks, quails and several nondescript

---

[8] Wikipedia, 2010, Biodiversity: Agriculture (en.wikipedia.org/wiki/Biodiversity# Agriculture).

populations.[9]

Marine and Coastal Biodiversity

India with a coastline of about 8,000 km, and an EEZ of 2.02 million sq km, shows a very wide range of coastal ecosystems like estuaries, lagoons, mangroves, backwaters, salt marshes, rocky coasts, and stretches and coral reefs, which are characterised by rich and unique biodiversity components (Venkataraman and Wafar 2005).[10] It is the third largest producer of fish in the world and the second largest producer of inland fish. As such, fisheries and aquaculture play an important role in social development, economic upliftment of farmers and fisherfolks, apart from contributing to the nutritional security of the country.

Fisheries in India, both capture and culture fisheries as also marine and freshwater fisheries witnessed phenomenal growth in last 6 decades. Marine fisheries remain one of the major items of export from India. Coastal aquaculture boomed and busted due to unsustainable use of coastal water but with regulatory control, the situation has changed. Marine exports from India rose by 10 per cent in 2008-09 because of an increase in production and rise in demand from China. India exported 6.02 lakh tonnes of seafood, showing an increase of 11.29 per cent in quantity and 12.95 per cent in earnings. China emerged as the second largest market, contributing 15 per cent to the total export of Rs.8607.94 crores, with the US, a close second at 12per cent. According to the Marine Products Export Development Authority, the European Union remained the largest market for Indian seafood accounting for 1,51,590 tonnes.[11] The exports grew largely because of increase in catch. Steps like GIS mapping in farm census and traceability would go a long way in increasing production.

Microbial Diversity

Microorganisms are well established and becoming increasingly significant

---

[9] India's Fourth National Report to the Convention on Biological Diversity, 2009. Ministry of Environment and Forests, Government of India, New Delhi

[10] Venkataraman and Wafar (2005), 'Coastal and Marine Biodiversity of India', Indian Journal of Marine Sciences, 34910:57-75.

[11] The Marine Products Export Development Authority, Ministry of Commerce and Industry, Government of India (www.mpeda.com)

in national economics. These are used for food production and preservation. such as production of antibiotics, making of oral contraceptives and other medicines, manufacture of vaccines, management of pests and pathogens, bioleaching of metals, increasing soil fertility, generating bio-fuels, creating perfumes, monitoring pollutants, ridding coal mines of methane, cleaning up of oil spills, waste water treatment, assaying of chemicals and serving as tools for medical research. In developing transgenic plants, microorganisms/ bacteria have become the source of genes, providing resistance to insects/ herbicides and enhancing productivity and quality of crops.

Forestry

India is endowed with vast forest resources. Forests play a vital role in social, cultural, historical, economic and industrial development of the country and in maintaining its ecological balance. They are the resource base for sustenance of its population and a storehouse of biodiversity. Other land use practices, such as agriculture and animal husbandry are benefitted by forests. Forests are increasingly being looked upon as major performers in poverty alleviation programmes. According to Global Forest Resource Assessment Report (Food and Agricultural Organisation (FAO) 2005), India ranks among the top ten countries in terms of forest area. India has 1.8 per cent of the global forest area with per capita forests of 0.08 ha. One noteworthy aspect in this regard, is the fact that against the prevailing global trend of decreasing forest cover, India has been successful in stabilising its area under forests.

Carbon Sequestration & Clean Development Management

The Kyoto Protocol, 1997, while setting the roadmap for implementation of UN Framework Convention on Climate Change, suggested Clean Development Management (CDM) to offset extra carbon emission. In simpler terms, one can encourage change over to green technology in order to save energy and reduce emission in a developing country and someone can buy the amount of Carbon Reduction Unit (CRU) in a virtual market to offset its own high emission rate. The other aspect of CDM is to encourage afforestation or reforestation of tropical land to increase carbon sink area and claim credit for such sequestration activities and trade it in open market. Global Carbon Market is continuously developing, starting from an almost nothing in 2003 to a multibillion dollar industry. The latest annual report from the World Bank on the global carbon market showed that in 2009, it grew to $144 billion, up 6per cent from 2008, despite enduring its most challenging year, to date.[12]

India and China are already acting as the major players in the Carbon Market. Business opportunities through investment in afforestation of degraded land can be seriously explored and with higher rate of carbon per tonne, the investment is likely to give good returns. Protecting standing forest, some experts feel, should be eligible for earning credit in future. That would serve better towards conservation of biodiversity. The Climate Community & Biodiversity Alliance (CCBA) is developing standards towards the objective of biodiversity benefit, while reducing carbon.[13]

Mangroves

Mangrove ecosystems constitute a bridge between terrestrial and marine ecosystems and are found in the inter-tidal zones of sheltered shores, estuaries, creeks, backwaters, lagoons, marshes and mud-flats and are regarded as most productive and biologically diverse ecosystems. Mangroves are habitats, spawning grounds, nurseries and nutrients for a number of animals. They harbour several endangered species, amphibians, mammals (tiger, deer, otter and dolphin) and birds (heron, egret, pelican and eagle). Only a few plant families (e.g. Rhizophoraceae, Avicenniaceae and Combretaceae) have developed physiological and structural adaptations to the brackish water habitat where mangroves occur. Mangroves in India account for about 5 per cent of the world's mangrove vegetation and are spread over an area of 4,445 km along the coastal states/UTs of the country. West Bengal has the maximum of mangrove cover in the country, followed by Gujarat and Andaman & Nicobar Islands.

Biotechnology

The biotech sector in India is among the fastest growing, knowledge-based sectors. The Indian biotech industry in 2008-09 registered 18 per cent

---

[12] State and Trends of the Carbon Market, 2010 (www.carbonfinance.org).
[13] Confronting Climate Change - Helping Communities Conserving Biodiversity (www.climate-standard.org).

growth, with record revenues of Rs.12,137 crores. The exports business went up by almost 25 per cent to Rs.7,152 crores, accounting for 60 per cent of the total business, in 2008-09. The domestic business at Rs.4,985 crores registered 10 per cent growth. The bio-pharma segment continued to account for the largest share of the biotech industry revenues. In 2008-09, the bio-pharma sector had a 65 per cent share of the total pie with revenues of $1.67 billions. The bio-services sector had 28 per cent share in exports (Rs.1,964 crores) registering a growth of 31 per cent. The bio-agri sector grew by 24 per cent to Rs.1,494 crores, the bioindustrial sector grew by 16 per cent to Rs.478 crores, and the bioinformatics sector grew by 15 per cent to amass Rs.220 crores, in revenues.[14]

Biofuel

Table 3-Export Share of Different Sectors, 2008-09

Sector	2008-09		2007-08	
	Exports (Rs Crore)	Percentage Share (%)	Exports (Rs Crore)	Percentage Share (%)
BioPharma	4,868	68.06	3,999	69.76
BioServices	1,964	27.46	1,502	26.20
BioAgri	61	0.85	51	0.90
BioIndustrial	89	1.24	30	0.52
Bioinformatics	170	2.38	150	2.62
Total	7,152	100	5,733	100

Increasing price and depleting oil reserves on one side and carbon emission from automobile fuel on the other, prompted scientists and policy makers to explore new and renewable fuel sources. Biofuel is a direct outcome of that effort. Sugarcane based ethanol is now becoming a part of blending in, in India. Jatropha plantation opened up new opportunities to produce bio-diesel. Chattisgarh has taken the lead and other states are keen to explore the new environment friendly fuel, which in turn, opens up business prospects in the era of climate change and global warming. Keeping land

---

[14] India in Business, Ministry of External Affairs, GoI (www. Indiainbusiness .nic. in).

for food crop, bio-fuel plantation in degraded land can offer enormous possibility for new business ventures.

Herbal Wealth

India has diverse agro climatic systems with over 17000-18000 species of flowering plants of which 6000-7000 are estimated to have medicinal usage in folk and documented systems of medicine, like Ayurveda, Siddha, Unani and Homoeopathy. About 960 species of medicinal plants are estimated to be in trade, of which 178 species have annual consumption levels in excess of 100 metric tonnes. Medicinal plants are not only a major resource base for the traditional medicines and herbal industry but also provide livelihood and health security to a large segment of Indian population. The domestic trade of the AYUSH industry is of the order of $1.5 to 2.0 billions. The Indian medicinal plants and their products also account for exports in the range of $ 200 millions. There is global resurgence in traditional and alternative health care systems, resulting in world herbal trade, which stands at US$ 120 billions and is expected to reach $ 7 trillions by 2050.[15]

Biodiversity in Totality

The economics of biodiversity is a newly emerging area of study. It has opened up scope for analysing current uses of bioresources in terms of business, as also potential for the future. The bioresources based product, when value added, can offer excellent returns in food, pharmaceutical, cosmetic, textile, fuel and other products. It is estimated that, at least three sectors like 'Certified Agriculture & Fisheries', 'Carbon Sequestration through Forestry and Bioprospecting' which may be relevant to India are likely to reach from $21 to 60 billions, $100 to $1,500 millions, $17.5 millions to $ 35 millions respectively between 2008 and 2010. By 2050 each of these three sectors is likely to show quantum jump. India can, at least share a part of this enormous potential market.

---

[15] National Medicinal Plants Board, Ministry of Health and Family Welfare. Department of AYUSH (nmpb.nic.in/index.php).

Table 4- Economic Benefits of Biodiversity Assets

• Percentage of pharmaceutical sector's turnover ($650 billions annually) derived from genetic resource: 20 to 50%	• Sixty percent of ecosystem services have been degraded in fifty years and the cost of failure to halt biodiversity loss on land alone, in lst 10 years, is estimated to be $500 billions.
• Namibia's protected areas contribute 6% of GDP, in tourism alone, with a significant potential for growth. Income from Namibia's conservancies (and conservancy- related activities): $ 4.1 millions. Percentage of total export from foreign tourist spending: estimated 24%.	• Giga tonnes of carbon stored in Canadian national parks: 4.43 (billion metric tonnes). Value of this service: $ 11bn - $ 2.2 trillions, depending on the market price of carbon.
• Contribution of the Great Barrier Reef to the Australian economy (value of tourism, other recreational activities and commercial fishing): AU$ 6 billions.	• Years of Mexico's 2004 carbon dioxide emissions offset by its protected areas: more than 5. Value of this service: $ 12.2 billions.
LIVELIHOODS AND EMPLOYMENT	
• Nearly a sixth of the world's population depends on protected areas for significant percent of their livelihoods.	• Wetlands of Okavango Delta generate $32 million per year to local households of Botswana, mainly through tourism. Total economic output: $ 145 millions - 2.6% of Botswana GNP.
• Over a billion people in developing countries, rely on fish ,as a major source of food and 80% of the world fisheries are fully or partially overexploited.	• Number of people in the world who rely on timber and non-timber forest products: 1.6 billions and annual rate of deforestation: 13 million hectares (or roughly the area of Bangladesh).
• Cost of global network of marine protected areas conserving 20-30% of the world's seas: up to $9 billion, annually creating around one million jobs.	

HEALTH, NUTRITION AND VULNERABILITY	
• Percentage of people in Africa estimated by WHO to rely on traditional medicines (plants and animals) as the main source of their health care needs: 80%	• About 8% of the 52,000 medicinal plants used today are threatened with extinction.
• Number of people worldwide who depend on drugs derived from forest plants for their medicinal needs: 1 billion.	

Source: www.cbd.int/2010

Ecotourism

Ecotourism can generate significant local economic benefit; build better management capacity and business skill and activity involving local communities in planning and management of such ventures. In India, ecotourism is growing rapidly with participation of the private sector. A recent study shows that in West Bengal, the growth of ecotourism in northern forested area of 'Gorumara' sanctuary vies with the southern mangrove haven in 'Sundarbans'. Tourism around biodiversity rich areas offers excellent opportunities for investment; such promotion can benefit the investor and help protect biodiversity and income generation at the local level. The trend of ecotourism shows that given the right infrastructural support, people, at large, are willing to pay for non-consumptive use of bioresources or for existence value of keystone species. The nature-tourism is increasing significantly in all well managed, protected areas system or in focussed ecosystems, like the backwater in Kerala. Corporate sectors, except a few, are yet to come up with investment, for promoting ecotourism to such destinations. It will be worthwhile to undertake market research for potential of expanding the ecotourism sector. According to Travel Weekly, sustainable tourism could grow to 25 per cent of the world's travel market by 2012, taking the value of the sector to approximately $473 billions a year.[16]

Biological Diversity Act and its Implementation

The Government of India has enacted the Biological Diversity Act in 2002, which provides for reaffirming sovereign rights over the biodiversity, regulation of conservation and sustainable use of biodiversity and associated

[16] United Nations World Tourism Organisation, "2020 Vision" (www.unwto.org).

knowledge. In order to implement the provisions of the Biodiversity Act, the National Biodiversity Authority (NBA) has been established in 2003, in Chennai. It is a corporate body, established by the Ministry of Environment and Forests, Government of India, to implement regulatory, advisory and monitoring roles for implementation of the Act. The implementation of BD Act is operated through decentralized regulation of activities, through local management committees, State biodiversity boards and the National Biodiversity Authority, each with well-defined functions within their respective jurisdiction. Accordingly, it is being implemented at national, state and local levels, as a three tier system. It places emphasis on meeting its objectives by involving different stakeholders in public, private and NGO sectors. To accelerate the process of implementation of the act, NBA is working closely with taxonomists, researchers, stakeholders and other Government departments for the conservation of the biological resources.

Conclusion

Biological Diversity has great economical potential; major part of it remains unexplored. In the current scenario, it is under threat and a good number of species is already in the list of endangered ones. The most important threats to biodiversity, for long, were habitat loss, due to large scale conversion of land to agriculture and urban centres, introduction of invasive alien species, and overexploitation of natural resources and pollution.

India, with a strong commitment to contribute towards achieving the 2010 target, is making concerted efforts, to significantly reduce the current rate of biodiversity loss. India has implemented National Biodiversity Action Plan, enacted acts, policies, missions and national actions towards conserving and managing the biodiversity. India's overall progress on all three objectives of the Convention on Biological Diversity has been commendable, considering the analysis of the achievements made towards the conservation of biodiversity. There is an urgent need to spread bio-literacy and bring on bio-happiness in biodiversity-rich areas. There should be strong alliance between people and the public sector, to address the issue. It is our bound duty and with conviction we should commit ourselves to champion the cause of converting "Biodiversity hot spots" to promising "biodiversity happy spots." Much has been said and written and it is time to ponder and act fast to conserve and sustainably use bio-wealth and associated traditional knowledge.

Ajit Kumar Singh

Regional Disparities in the post- Reform Period

Introduction

Independent India inherited a backward and regionally imbalanced economy, reflecting the distorted pattern of development, imposed by the colonial power, to subserve its own interests. Most of the industrial and commercial activities were concentrated in the three metropolitan centres, namely, Bombay, Calcutta and Madras and a few major cities like Ahmedabad, Kanpur and Delhi. Most of the other areas of the country remained in the backwaters of underdevelopment.

Removal of the existing regional disparities was therefore a major challenge before the policy makers. Rightfully, balanced regional development has been one of the important objectives of economic planning in the country since the very beginning. A large battery of policy instruments was pressed into service to achieve the objective of balanced regional development. These included larger flow of resources in favour of the poorer states, location of public sector projects in the backward areas, capital and transport subsidies to industrially backward areas, etc. (see for details Ajit Kumar Singh 1981, Ch. 1). In due course of time, several area-based programmes were adopted for the development of geographically handicapped regions like Drought Prone Area Development Programme, Desert Development Programmes, Hill Area Development Programme and Tribal Area Development Programme. Horizontal equity among states was also given priority in resource transfers to the states, both by the Finance Commissions and the Planning Commission.

In several earlier studies, the present author has examined the impact of the government policies and measures on inter-state disparities in the

Country (Ajit Kumar Singh 1984, 1992, 1999). It was found that disparities declined in the fifties, but showed a divergent trend in the sixties (Ajit Kumar Singh 1984). The process of divergence continued in the seventies, but it seemed to have been arrested in the early eighties (Ajit Kumar Singh 1992).

The study of the experience of the first four decades of development planning in India, led the present author to conclude that "Development planning did succeed in breaking the long standing barriers to growth and initiating a geographically wide spread process of growth, throughout the country. Though it has not been able to fully reverse the process of spatially uneven development, it has definitely slowed down the inherent economic tendency towards increased regional imbalances" (Ajit Kumar Singh 1992).

Impact of Economic Reforms

The economic reforms initiated in India from 1991 brought about a paradigm change in the economic policy regime. The policy of state led and directed development gave place to market-led growth. The regulatory mechanism which was under operation for the last four decades was gradually dismantled and a policy of liberalisation of domestic and external market was adopted. This led to the withdrawal of state from several important sectors of the economy and greater reliance on private capital, both domestic and foreign, to spur economic growth in the country. Thus, we find that the share of public investment, which exceeded 60 per cent of total investment in the earlier plans, has gradually come down to 22 per cent in the Eleventh Five Year Plan.

The fiscal crisis which widely characterised the budgets of the central and the state governments, affected the capacity of the government to invest in productive activities or economic and social infrastructure, where again public-private partnership mode was adopted. The backward states were particularly handicapped in this respect.

The main public instruments, like provisions for establishing public sector projects in backward regions, capital subsidy and other financial incentives for investment in backward areas etc., which were used in the pre-reform era, to direct the flow of public and private investments in favour of the backward states and regions, were withdrawn. The financial sector reforms too led to the dilution of social objectives behind the flow of credit to backward regions and priority sectors. The states were also persuaded to remove the concessions that they had offered, to attract industry to their respective states.

In the new policy regime, private investment began to flow to the regions which yielded higher profits, rather than the regions that needed higher investment. The richer states, with better infrastructure, attracted more private investment to the detriment of the poorer states.

From the very beginning of the reform process, economists expressed the apprehension that the new economic policies would promote a regionally more concentrated pattern of investment and growth which would aggravate regional disparities in the country. This led to renewed interest in the issue of regional disparities and a number of articles and studies came out in the nineties and the present decade, seeking to examine whether growth is leading to regional convergence or divergence (Ahluwalia, 2000; Bhattacharya and Saktivel, 2004; Gupta and Kalra, 2005; Singh, 1999).

Flow of Private Investment

The actual pattern of investment flow in the post-reform period, confirms the apprehension of the economists that the new liberal economic policies would lead to a concentrated pattern of investment, in favour of the richer states. Table 1 shows the state-wise distribution of proposed investment through IEMs (Industrial Entrepreneurs Memorandum). During the period 1991-2001, almost 68 per cent of the proposed investment, went to the eight richest states of India. Only three states, namely, Maharashtra, Gujarat and Andhra Pradesh cornered half of the investment. Among the poorer states, the share of UP and MP was about 7 per cent each, much below their share in population. Rajasthan's share was about 4 per cent, while Orissa got only 2.3 per cent and Bihar, a paltry 1.4 per cent.

Table 1: State-wise Investment Proposed through Industrial Entrepreneurs'

Memorandum during Reform Period (1991-2009)

States (in Descending Order Per Capita GSDP)	1991-2001		2001-2009		1991-2009	
	Investment (Rs. Crore)	% of Total Investment	Investment (Rs. Crore)	% of Total Investment	Investment (Rs. Crore)	% of Total Investment
Haryana	28423	3.00	47892	1.00	76315	1.33
Maharashtra	205431	21.72	342995	7.13	548426	9.53
Kerala	7959	0.84	2842	0.06	10801	0.19
Punjab	38189	4.04	54209	1.13	92398	1.61
Gujarat	157491	16.65	567297	11.80	724788	12.59
Tamil Nadu	56512	5.97	204560	4.25	261072	4.54
Karnataka	43759	4.63	404639	8.41	448398	7.79
Andhra Pradesh	105467	11.15	392737	8.17	498204	8.66
West Bengal	31681	3.35	259851	5.40	291532	5.07
Rajasthan	37426	3.96	66436	1.38	103862	1.80
Orissa	21424	2.26	701823	14.59	723247	12.57
Jharkhand			388737	8.08	388737	6.75
Madhya Pradesh	66878	7.07*	300843	6.26	367721	6.39
Uttar Pradesh	71515	7.56*	120319	2.50	191834	3.33
Bihar	13436	1.42*	28145	0.59	41581	0.72
India	945965	100	4809369	100.00	5755334	100.00

*Refers to the undivided State.

Source: Website of the Ministry for Industries, Govt. of India.

During the current decade, there was some improvement in the pattern of investment in terms of its spatial spread. The share of the top 8 states came down to 42 per cent from 68 per cent, in the previous decade. The share of Maharashtra, Gujarat and Andhra Pradesh, which attracted the largest investment in the previous decade, declined markedly in this period. The main gainers were the states of Orissa and Jharkhand. These states are richly endowed with mineral resources, which attracted heavy investment. However, other poor states like UP, Rajasthan and Bihar show a dismal situation in this respect. However, taking the entire post-reform period (1991-2009), the pattern of investment has remained highly skewed in favour of the richer states. About 31 per cent of the total investment in the post-reform period has gone to Gujarat, Maharashtra and Orissa. On the other hand, the share of the poorest six states, excluding Orissa, is a meagre 20 per cent.

Fiscal Transfers to States

There are marked differences in the fiscal capacity of the states. The poorer states are unable to raise sufficient revenue from their tax and non-tax resources, to provide for the required level of public services to their people. These fiscal imbalances are also reflected in the differences in per capita expenditure of the states. Srivastava has found that per capita expenditure level is substantially below the average in Bihar, Uttar Pradesh and Madhya Pradesh, while it is more than 50 per cent of the average expenditure in Punjab, Maharashtra and Gujarat (Srivastava, 2005, p. 294). Given the large variations in per capita public expenditure at the state level, differences in the availability and quality of public services, are bound to exist.

The Finance Commissions were expected to address the problem of vertical and horizontal imbalances in the fiscal system. Horizontal equity has been an important consideration in the awards accorded by the successive Finance Commissions. However, a close scrutiny of the devolutions by the Finance Commissions, reveals that they have not been able to do full justice to the issue. In fact, the post-devolution surpluses have been modest in amount, in per capita terms. But a more glaring failure of the Finance Commission awards is that the post-devolution surplus shows a strong positive association with the level of per capita income of the states (Ajit

Kumar Singh, 2008). A very perceptive observer of Indian public finances has observed that transfers by the Finance Commissions have failed to remove the disparities in the revenue capacities of the states in any substantial measure (Bagchi 2005, p. 3395). As pointed out by him, the capita revenue capacity of the richer states, like Punjab, Haryana and Maharashtra is almost double that of the poorer states, like Uttar Pradesh and Bihar.

In short, the generous transfers by the Finance Commissions have failed to remove disparities in revenue capacities of the states in any substantial measure. This means that not only are the quality and level of public services and infrastructure, much better in the richer states, their capacity for investment expenditure is also higher and they are in a better position to get more funds from the Planning Commission and attract more private investments. It is this complexity that lies at the root of the persistent and growing inter-regional disparities, at the state level in the country. The system of fiscal transfers in the country must therefore address this imbalance, taking into account, the totality of the flows.

What is a more serious matter of concern is that total governmental transfers now constitute a rather small and declining part of the total financial flows in the economy. The share of gross fiscal transfers from the Central Government to the states, which amounted to a little less than one-fourth of the total financial transfers in the early 1990s, has come down to around one-sixth in recent years (Ajit Kumar Singh, 2008). Thus, in the post-reform scenario, the inter-governmental fiscal transfers are now completely dwarfed by the flows through financial institutions. The main determinant of economic growth in the changed scenario is private investment, which tends to go in favour of the richer states as we have shown above. However, Finance Commissions' devolutions remain important, particularly for the poorer states, that have a limited resource base of their own and are also unable to attract sufficient resources from other financial channels.

Trends in Inter-State Disparities Since 1991

Given the pattern of skewed investment and resource flow observed during the last two decades, one would expect that the pattern of growth has

Table 2: Trend Growth Rate in GSDP during 1980s and 1990s

State	Per Capita GSDP in Rs.(Average for 1999-200-2)	1980-81 to 1989-90	1990-91 to 2001-02	2002--03 to 2008--09	Change in Percent Points (4) over (3)	Change in Percent Points (5)over (4)
1	2	3	4	5	6	7
Punjab	28030	5.44	4.66	6.00	-0.78	1.34
Maharashtra	26994	5.64	6.27	7.07	0.63	0.80
Haryana	26256	6.21	4.72	9.09	-1.49	4.37
Kerala	22824	3.16	5.51	8.27	2.35	2.76
Gujarat	22708	5.05	7.2	10.75	2.15	3.55
Tamil Nadu	22587	5.18	6.26	6.12	1.08	-0.14
Karnataka	20703	5.36	7.17	8.63	1.81	1.46
Andhra Pradesh	18869	5.35	5.6	9.09	0.25	3.49
West Bengal	17377	4.70	6.93	7.14	2.23	0.21
Rajasthan	15059	6.01	5.85	10.14	-0.16	4.29
Madhya Pradesh	13340	4.02	4.81	6.16	0.79	1.35
Orissa	11234	5.01	4.21	10.95	-0.8	6.74
Uttar Pradesh	10798	4.80	3.84	6.12	-0.96	2.28
Bihar	6539	4.60	3.79	9.08	-0.81	5.29

Source: Column 2, 3 and 4 have been taken from CSO estimates as reported in the Twelfth Finance Commission Report, p. 58. Growth rates for 2002-09 have been calculated from CSO estimates of GSDP.

been uneven across states. Table 2 shows the state-wise growth rate of GSDP in the pre- and post-reform period. During the eighties, the differences in growth rates of Gross State Domestic Product (GSDP) in different states were not very marked. However, growth rates of GSDP in the poorer states decelerated in the 1990s, as compared to the 1980s, while the growth rates accelerated in the richer states. All the poor states, except Madhya Pradesh, witnessed lower economic growth in the nineties, as compared to the eighties. Among the richer states, Haryana and Punjab show a relative slowdown in their rates of growth during this period, though their growth rates are still fairly high. The main gainers of higher growth in the nineties were the states of Kerala, West Bengal, Gujarat, Karnataka, Tamil Nadu and Madhya Pradesh. All these states, with the exception of Madhya Pradesh, belong to high or medium per capita income category. The coefficient of correlation between per capita State Domestic Product (SDP) and growth rate of GSDP was 0.5 during the nineties, indicating that the richer states have grown faster than the poorer states, during this period.

During the last decade, all the states, except Tamil Nadu have witnessed faster growth, as compared to the nineties. The jump in growth rate was quite marked in some of the poor states, e.g. Bihar, Orissa, Rajasthan and UP. This indicates that there has been some catching up, on the part of the lagging states, in recent years. In fact, the coefficient of correlation between per capita SDP and growth rate of GSDP was -0.19, showing better performance of the poor states, in recent years.

While the growth rate of GSDP has been slower in the poorer states, population growth has been faster in these states. As a result, the increase in per capita income has been slower. Not surprisingly, indicators of inter-state disparities in per capita SDP like minimum-maximum ratio and coefficient of variation, show a clear worsening of the situation in the 1990s as observed by the Twelfth Finance Commission, in its report. Bihar has remained the poorest state of the country throughout this period, while Punjab (in some years Maharashtra) had the highest per capita income. The ratio of minimum to maximum declined from 30.53 per cent in 1993-94 to 28.90 per cent 1999-00. The coefficient of variation in per capita income jumped in this period from 34.55 per cent to 37.42 per cent (Table 3).

Table 3: Trends in Inter-State Disparity in Per Capita GSDP: 1993-2000

Year	State with lowest per capita GSDP	State with highest per capita GSDP	Ratio of Minimum to Maximum per capita GSDP (%)	Coefficient of variation(%)
1993-94	Bihar	Punjab	30.53	34.55
1994-95	Bihar	Punjab	29.70	35.03
1995-96	Bihar	Punjab	26.11	37.89
1996-97	Bihar	Maharashtra	27.59	36.78
1997-98	Bihar	Maharashtra	28.28	35.93
1998-99	Bihar	Maharashtra	30.02	35.90
1999-00	Bihar	Maharashtra	28.90	37.42

Note: Based on CSO data. Relates to 14 states, i.e. Assam and the general category states, excluding Goa.

Source: Twelfth Finance Commission Report, p.59.

The trend towards worsening of the inter-state income disparity has continued unabated in the present decade. Haryana emerged as the state with highest per capita income, while Bihar remained at the bottom. The minimum-maximum ratio declined sharply from 30.0 per cent in 2001-02 to 20.4 per cent in 2007-08. Coefficient of variation in per capita SDP also maintained the upward trend, throughout the period.

Table 4: Trends in Inter-State Disparity in Per Capita GSDP: 2000-2009

Year	State with lowest per capita GSDP	State with highest per capita GSDP	Ratio of Minimum to Maximum per capita GSDP (%)	Coefficient of variation (%)
2001-02	Bihar	Punjab	30.02	34.78
2002-03	Bihar	Haryana	28.90	36.06
2003-04	Bihar	Haryana	22.71	35.93

2004-05	Bihar	Haryana	20.11	36.18
2005-06	Bihar	Haryana	20.38	37.13
2006-07	Bihar	Haryana	21.89	37.77
2007-08	Bihar	Haryana	21.87	38.31

Note: Based on CSO data. Data relates to the 16 general category states, excluding Goa.
Source: Calculated from CSO data, based on 1999-2000 constant prices.

Demand for Creation of New States

As the above analysis shows, the inter-state economic disparities have sharply risen in the post-reform period. Therefore, the issue of regional disparities has once again emerged as a major concern of the Indian political economy. While the Indian economy has moved on to a higher growth path, the pattern of growth has been regionally concentrated and many regions have been by-passed in the race towards higher economic growth. It is this uneven pattern of growth that lies behind the demands for the creation of separate states, emanating from different regions of the country. These regional pressures have led to the creation of three separate states of Uttarakhand, Chhatisgarh and Jharkhand, which were created in 2000, by bi-furcating the erstwhile states of Uttar Pradesh, Madhya Pradesh and Bihar. Similar demands are emerging from several other regions of the country, e.g. Bundelkhand, Telangana and Vidharbha.

A valid question that arises in this context is whether the creation of new and smaller states will be desirable in the national interest and whether that will help in promoting faster development in the lagging regions. The author is of the view that the feelings of regional identity, if channelised along healthy lines, can provide a powerful force to mobilise people of a region, for regional and national development. It would be appropriate to quote the views of the State Reorganisation Commission, 1955 on this issue. The Commission recognised the positive role of regionalism and observed as follows:

"......a regional consciousness, not merely in the sense of a negative
awareness of absence of repression or exploitation but also in the sense
of scope for positive expression of the collective personality of a people

inhabiting a state or a region, may be conducive to the contentment
and well-being of the community" (Report of the State Reorganisation
Commission, 1955, p. 255).

Dr. B.R. Ambedkar, commenting on the report of the State
Reorganisation Commission, supported the idea of smaller states in the
following words:

> "As the area of the state increases, the proportion of the minority to the
> majority (communities/castes) decreases and the position of the
> minority (castes) becomes precarious and opportunities for the majority
> to practise tyranny over the minority become greater. The States must
> therefore be small "(as reported in Hindustan Times, New Delhi Feb.
> 2, 2010, p, 9).

He gave the following criteria for division of a linguistic state: "Into
how many states people speaking one language should be cut up, should
depend upon (1) the requirement of efficient administration, (2) the needs
of the different areas, (3) the sentiments of the different areas, and (4) the
proportion between the majority and the minority" (as reported in
Hindustan Times, New Delhi Feb. 2, 2010, p. 9)."

There is a strong case for another reorganisation of the Indian states
into smaller units, based on objective criteria. The states of UP, Maharashtra,
Rajasthan, Andhra Pradesh etc. are too large to be governed efficiently.
Splitting of these states into smaller units will be beneficial for the people
of all the regions. The smaller states will also be administratively more
manageable. This will definitely improve the efficiency and improve the
quality of delivery of public services. The smaller states will be able to plan
for the development of their area and people, more effectively, in the light
of region-specific resources and problems. They would also be in a better
position to attract more private investment for their development, as the
experience of the newly created states of Uttaranchal, Chhattisgarh and
Jharkhand, have shown. These states have also shown an upsurge in their
growth rates, after their creation. This was also the experience of
reorganisation of the erstwhile Punjab into three smaller states of Punjab,

Himachal Pradesh and Haryana.

Political sagacity demands that a rational and objective view of these issues is taken and timely action initiated, instead of waiting till the time when the situation takes a violent turn, as has happened in Andhra Pradesh recently. It is high time that the Central government appoints a Second State Reorganisation Commission.

References

Ahluwalia, M.S. (2000), 'Economic Performance of States in Post Reform Period,' *Economic and Political Weekly,* May 6, Vol. 35, No. 19.

Bhattacharya, B.B. and Saktivel, S. (2004), 'Forecasting Regional Growth and Disparity in India: Comparison of Pre and Post-Reform Decades', *Economic and Political Weekly,* Vol. 39, No. 10.

Bagchi, Amaresh, 'Symposium on Report of Twelfth Finance Commission: Introduction and Overview', *Economic and Political Weekly*, Vol. XL, No. 31, 2005.

Government of India (1955), Report of the State Reorganisation Commission, New Delhi.

Gupta, J.R. and Kalra, Manjit (2005), "Federal Transfers and Inter-State Disparities in India", Atlantic Publishers & Distributors, New Delhi.

Hindustan Times, New Delhi, February 2, 2010.

Singh, Ajit Kumar (1981), "Patterns of Regional Development: A Comparative Study", Sterling Publishers, New Delhi.

_____(1984), "Trends in Regional Disparities", *Productivity,* Vol.35, No.2, July-September.

_____(1992), "Regional Dualism, Regionalism and Development Process in India", *In Search of India's Renaissance,* Centre for Research in Rural and Industrial Development, Chandigarh.

_____(1999), "Inter-State Disparities in Per Capita SDP in India: Trends and Causes," *Arth Vigyan*, Vol.51, No.2.

_____(2008), 'Finance Commission Devolutions and Regional Imbalances', in Singh, Ajit Kumar (ed.) "Twelfth Finance Commission Recommendations and their Implications for the State Finances, APH, New Delhi.

Srivastava, D.K. (2005), "Issues in India Pubic Finances", New Century Publications, New Delhi.

Ashutosh Mishra

Religion-Politics Interface: Primordial Politics in Nigerian Context

The ferocity and frequency of religious violence has marked Nigeria as Africa's new trouble-spot. For Nigeria, the year 2010 has started in the ominous backdrop of Abdulmuttalik's arrest in December and before that, the ultra-atavistic rebellion of Boko Haram in July, last year. Then January, this year, saw unprecedented level of religious violence in Jos - the Capital city of Plateau province. This city seems to have an insatiable thirst for blood, as every riot seems to be succeeded by another riot here, the next being bloodier than the preceding one. The ambient hatred has culminated in major riots here in December 2008 and January-March 2010. Perhaps Muslims were the aggrieved party of the January-February 2010 riot and thus they triggered this almost genocidal level of violence in the next month.

These incidents have very categorical global repercussions also. For instance, the Vatican has officially condemned Jos riots and has demanded rehabilitation and reasonable redressal of grievances of local Christians. Colonel Gaddafi, in his trade-mark foot-in-the-mouth statement, has recommended division of Nigeria, along religious lines. Thus coastal, riverine and tropical rain-forest regions of Christian dominated south will be separated from Sahel, Savanna and plateau regions of the Muslim-dominated north. Naturally, his gratuitous advice has created a diplomatic row.

Because of the demographic, territorial and economic strength, Nigeria's religious violence is a cause of inter-continental concern. These violent events have shattered the western world's dream of turning Nigeria into a peaceful oil-rich alternative of the troubled emirate states. "The next Gulf"[1] potential of Nigeria is now buried deep. The West, particularly

---

[1]Rowel, Andy (2005), "Raging Battles against Energy Giants in Nigeria", The Guardian, article republished in The Times of India, 10 Nov.

America, is worried about losing Nigeria to religious extremism, because Nigeria is "most populous and except for small areas in Congo, the most densely populated African nation."[2] That's why various scholars have described Nigeria as the "Giant of Africa,"[3] "a Territorial colossus,"[4] "Africa's Goliath"[5] and "a natural leader of black Africa"[6]. Her oil-revenue gives her the second largest GDP in the sub-Saharan Africa.[7] That's why Nigeria's demographic and economic strength, makes her religious politics, an international issue.

Refusal to Recognise the Public Role of Religion

Religion, undoubtedly, has always held a pivotal position in Nigerian politics but now it appears to have acquired a more assertive and aggressive role and carries the potential of destroying the territorial integrity of the country. John Hunwick argues that because of this fear, most scholars have refused to recognise the public role of religion.[8] In this ostrich-like wilful avoidance of religion in political discourse, Nigerian scholars were well-synchronised with contemporary hegemonic academic approaches. As Kenneth Wald has shown, Western Political Science followed it mindlessly.[9] The 'religion-blindness' of Political Science was caused by the prevalence of secularisation and modernisation theories, a sense of disinterest (if not hatred) towards religion, a general assumption of religion being retrogressive, detachment of academicians from the real world and elitist arrogance of liberal

---

[2] Land, Harry (1961), 'Nigeria' in Colin Legum (ed.) "The Africa Handbook", p. 211, Anthony Blond Ltd., London.

[3] ibid, p. 211

[4] Adameoyega, Wale (1962), "The Federation of Nigeria", p. 6, George G. Harrap, London.

[5] Hatch, John (1970), "Nigeria : A History", p. 09, Seckar and Warburg, London.

[6] Dasgupta, Punyapriya (1995), "Tyranny in Nigeria Fuelled by Oil", The Times of India, 20 Nov.

[7] Petroleum in Nigeria, Wikipedia article.

[8] Hunwick, John (1992), "Nigeria: An African Case Study of Political Islam", p.155, Annals, AAPSS, Nov.

"In fact, the religion question in one form or another has been an integral part of Nigerian Political discourse, since the beginning of party politics. Most constitutional and political thinking has refused to face this stark fact, mainly for fear of animosity that might be stirred up".

[9] Wald, Kenneth and Wilcox, Cylyde (2006), "Getting Religion : Has Political Science Rediscovered the Faith Factor? American Political Science Review, Vol. 100, No. 4, Nov.

[10] Pipes, Daniel (1983), "In the Path of God: Islam and Political Power", p.05, Basic Books, New York."To ignore religious desires and to concentrate only on the economic drives or secularized political motives is to limit unnecessarily scope of our understanding"- John Voll

establishments. Thus, political scientists were accustomed to explain every religious activity, solely by socio-economic factors.[10] For them, religion was an illusion, a surrogate and an alibi. Modern academics is dominated by Rawlsian ground-rule that "public reason" and not 'comprehensive doctrines" should be the legitimate universe of academic discourse and public policy.[11]

As Kenneth Wald has pointed out, the situation has started changing from 1980s but still religion is struggling hard to be recognised as an independent causal variable for political phenomena. There is one particular reason responsible for avoidance of religion, in secular African context. As pointed out by David Robinson, historically Islamic cultures of Africa were studied within the orientalist framework, which was considered to be different from, and not integrally related to, the African studies.[12] This erroneous separation between black African and Islamic identities is still widely accepted. For instance, Huntington categorises Magrib as part of Islamic civilization but considers sub-Saharan Africa as an autonomous black civilization.[13]

Huntington's omnibus category of black civilization hides a very critical division within Nigeria and other West African states. While Sahel, Savanna and Plateau regions of Northern Nigeria are, integral parts of the great

---

[10] Pipes, Daniel (1983), "In the Path of God: Islam and Political Power", p.05, Basic Books, New York. "To ignore religious desires and to concentrate only on the economic drives or secularized political motives is to limit unnecessarily scope of our understanding"- John Voll
[11] Sweetman, Branden (2006), "Why Politics Needs Religion: The Place of Religious Arguments in the Public Square", IVP Academics, Illinois. Other relevant works are-
(a) George, Robert, (2001), "Clash of Orthodoxy: Law, Religion and Morality in Crisis", ISI Books, Wilmington, Delaware.
(b) Rawls, John (1996), "Political Liberalism", Columbia, University Press, New York.
(c) Greenwalt, Kent (1995), "Private Consciences and Public Reasons", Oxford University Press, New York.
(d) Dawkins, Richards (1987), "The Blind Watchmaker", Norton, New York. .
[12] Robinson, David (2004), "Muslim Societies in African History", Cambridge University Press. "One of Robinson's primary objective is to bridge the ancient schism between the study of Islam and the study of Africa brought about by the isolated development of the respective disciplines of oriental and African studies" - Rehma Bavelaar, The Myriad Paths of Islam in Africa, p.02, http:/www.islamonline.net.
[13] Huntington, Samuel P. (1996), "The Clash of Civilization and Remaking of World Order, Simon and Schuster, New York. Maps on p. 26-27.

Sudan, Negroid and Islamic civilization, occupying 10° to 16° of Northern latitudes,[14] the Coastal Delta and other parts of southern Nigeria are integrated to the vegetational and climatological zones of the their similar Northern latitudes. This bifurcates Nigerian identity into two distinct Islamic and Christian identities, who were mostly alien to each other until as late as nineteenth century and when they were brought together by Britishers, they turned antagonistic.

Coincidence of Ethnicity and Religion

There are certain reasons which have created much wider space for religion to intervene in African politics in regular, legitimate and decisive ways. Some reasons are peculiar to Nigeria while others can be counted as common to several other African states as well. Some important ascriptive and historical factors were naturally inherited by the independent Nigerian state. First and foremost of those, is the coincidence of religion with ethnicity. Even in normal circumstances, as Jeff Haynes notes, "it is often difficult to separate ethnicity and religion, as both are essential components of a nation's self-identify.[15] Because of the coincidence of these two critical cultural bench-mark identities of Nigeria, it was easy to interpret various encounters between different Nigerian communities as mainly ethnically-driven rather than religion-oriented, though the role of religion was unmistakable.[16] This explanatory format was somewhat natural. Analysts were also under peer pressure and fearful of rejection if they happened to emphasise religion in their writings. Very few scholars could see this

---

[14] Trimingham, J. Spencer (1961), 'Islam in Africa', in Colin Legum (ed.) "Africa Handbook", p.478, Anthony Bland Ltd., London.--Trimingham calls West Africa's compact Muslim dominated areas (including Northern Nigeria) as "The third belt" of Africa's Muslim community, which is conservative because of "relative isolation from the main impact".

[15] Haynes, Jeff (2003), "Religion in Third World Politics", p.08, Open University Press, Buckingham.

[16] "Inter-Ethnic conflict in Nigeria has generally had a religious element. Riots against Igbo in 1953 and in the 1960s, in the north, were said to be fired by religious conflict. The riots against Igbo in the north, in 1966, were said to have been inspired by radio reports of mistreatment of Muslims in the south. In the 1980s, serious outbreaks between Christians and Muslims occurred in Kafanchan in Southern Kaduna State, in a border area between the two religions" - Religion in Nigeria, p.203, Wikipedia.

[17] Jeff Haynes is one of very few scholars who could see the ethnicity-religion fusion, and "increasing importance of ethnicity in politics from the late 1970s, often interacting with religion, as politically salient feature" - Jeff Haynes, op. cit., p. 06.

significant ethnic-religion fusion and factor that in their analyses of political events.[17] Only the global Islamic revival could change the mind-set of academicians and make religion, an extremely relevant explanatory variable.

Nigeria was virtually a confederal state during British rule. It was changed only in May 1967 when 12 federated provinces were created. In this confederal structure, three big regions had almost independent constitutional status; even their Prime Ministers and provinces were kept under their (regional) control. Northern region had two-thirds of total Muslim population of the country, south-east was also religiously almost homogeneous and only south-west had mixed population. These three regions were dominated by single ethnic communities of their regions. All these three regions had, in Pugh and Buchanan's terminology, "dual make-up."[18] Thus, Nigeria had six sub-regions. Of them, four - Hausaland, Igboland, C.O.R. and Mid-West were homogeneous while middle Belt and Yorubaland had mixed population. Thus regional and sub-regional ethnicity were coalescent with religion. This particular geographical, ethnological and colonial attribute, strengthened religious identities significantly.

The Historical and Colonial Context

During colonial times, Northern Nigeria was under local emirs who were Fulanis of Mali origin. Britishers allowed them to govern under Indirect Rule system. These Fulani clerics[19] had occupied the region by waging jihad against the local majority community of Hausa Muslims, during early decades of the nineteenth century. In fact, the Fulanic Ulema jihadism was an integral part of a massive puritanical wave which swept the whole of western Sudan at that time.[20] Sheikh Fodio was the most prominent of

---

[18] Pugh and Buchanan's classification is described in James S Coleman "Nigeria: Background to Nationalism", p. 329, University of California Press, Berkley, 1962.

[19] Trimingham, J. Spencer , op. cit., p.152-153 "The nineteenth century, however, was characterised by the emergence of a new type of militant Islam. Clerics appeared who waged jihad and formed a number of theocratic states in west African region.

[20] "The west African Jihads at this time were led by Muslim teachers or scholars, taking inspiration variously from earlier militant reformers" - Jeff Haynes, op.cit., p. 07

[21] "The most famous of them was Sheikh Uthman Ibn Fodi, who fought a revolutionary jihad against the lax Muslim rulers of Hausaland (Northern Nigeria) from 1804 to 1808 - "The History of Islam in Africa: A Historical Review", Zahrah Awaleh, p.02,   h t t p : / www.islamawareness.net/ Africa-P.02

those armed cleric campaigners.[21] His caliphate was the nucleus of these religious regimes.[22] These victorious Fulanis had only religious puritanism to legitimise their usurpation of power. This particular political interest turned Fulanis over-religious and demonstrative. They managed and even manipulated methodically, every instrument under their control, to ensure that education, judicial system, popular beliefs and even taxation of Northern emirates, were based on their sectarian (Mehadist, Qadiriya Sufi and Caliphal) interpretation of religion.[23] For Fulani emirs, their overlord Sardauna of Sokoto was the Caliph who had spiritual as well as temporal authority.

Thus in Northern Nigeria under Sardauna and emirs, religion was the sole criterion of every government action for about one and a half centuries. (The distinct North-West Borno state adopted the same policies under Shehu rulers). These emirs launched Northernisation campaign soon after independence, which was only a sugar-coated Islamisation campaign. The evangelical Christians of Middle Belt and Catholic Christians of South-East Nigeria followed suit in the same aggressive manner, sometimes in unintended imitation and sometimes as considered strategy. Since the Nigerian Constitution did not give any special protection to the Christian minority, Christians were worried and they felt justified in engaging in religion-driven politics. Independence brought mass participation, competition and populism in politics. A massive stake in the spoils of the system was created and lower common denominator kind of politics was encouraged. Religion became more pervasive and the perverse factor in Nigerian politics. The whole system became extremely vulnerable to religious

---

[22] "The Kunta, the Caliph of Masina and the Caliph of Sokoto came to dominate the commerce of Western Sudan. One scholar had described this commercial cooperation between the three centres of powers as giving rise to a Sokoto Common Market".- Mervyn Hiskett, "The Development of Islam in West Africa", Chapter "Sokoto Caliphate, and Hamdullahi Dina", p.179, Longman, London, 1984.

[23] Hiskett, Mervyn, p.170, op.cit."In Sokoto Caliphate, the ulemas were given considerable authority as quda (sing.- qadi), magistrates, and in other official capacities. Similarly, taxation was modelled according to Islamic practice. The conquered peoples were referred to as dhimmis, the non-Muslim subjects of the seventh century Arab empire and an attempt was made, to tax them according to the system evolved at that time. In their personal lives, the Sokoto Caliphs consciously tried to imitate the life-style of the partriarchal caliphs of the first Islamic century."

pressures. It remains so in civilian as well as in army mode of governance.

As indicated earlier, regional-ethnic and religious identities reinforce each other and thus make their presence very powerful. Nigerian's census operations give us a sense of disintegrative effects of these categories. After bitter experiences of 1962 and 1963 census, federal Government felt compelled to exclude religious category altogether from census proceedings. Because of religious (and regional- ethnic) factors, John Herkovits notes, "the taking of census had been critical, indeed a root cause of war in the past.[24] The census operations of 1962 and 1963[25] led "finally to the military coup in 1966 and the next year, to the civil war." In the census of December 1973, "soldiers accompanied enumerators and counter-signed the results." Keeping in view the explosive nature of census, "Government's advanced publicity stressed economic planning; purpose was not, it insisted, political." The army ruler also cautioned that results were provisional. In fact, he used provisional, nine times in one single broadcast and when final results came out, he remarked that these data are "even less than preliminary." The Nigerians were compelled to believe that "the only method by which the census could be conducted fairly and without dangerous acrimony would be for it to be supervised by foreigners."[26]

Religion as "Refuge and Political Weapon"

Nigeria is very atypical of neighbouring and even other African or Muslim-majority states in a very special way. Its case is very unique in the sense that perhaps it belongs to a category of very few states where modern ideologies of socialism, communism, liberalism, atheism and secularism could never get any recognisable influence even at ethereal elitist level. All these ideologies had some presence, sometimes symbolic and stratospheric and

---

[24] Herkovits, Jean (1974), "Nigeria : Africa's New Power", Foreign Affairs, p.132, Nov.

[25] Every region engaged in massive fraud by fictiously inflating their population. For instance "a town of 20 thousand people was discovered in the eastern region" - Yome Durotoye, "The role of Nigerian Parliament in the Disintegration of Nigeria's Political Regime : 1960-66", Indian Political Science Review, April, 1970.

[26] Hatch, John, op. cit., p. 256.

[27] Hollinger, Arnold (1981), 'Arab Communism at Low Ebb' in "Problem of Communism", July-August. The Arab Communists on occasion, in different countries at different times, have enjoyed a modest measure of success.

sometimes even substantial, in most of the African, Arab and Islamic states. Many Arab countries had even strong communist parties,[27] while Destourian and Bath variants of socialism were ideologies of several Arab, Muslim and African regimes. These ideologies have usually worked as a bulwark against excessive influence of religion in politics. Sometimes at least trade unions provided for these ideologies, some popular base. Strangely and rather unfortunately, these ideologies could not get even moderate base in Nigeria. Thus religion became quite a formidable force in Nigerian politics, also by default as well.

Of all these ideologies, secularism is the most relevant one in the present context of religion-politics interface. Even formal and nominal secularism was absent in Nigeria's political discourses and the constitutional system did not subscribe to it. As John Paden writes, "Nigeria remains a multi-religious rather than a secular society."[28] Regimes routinely take care to earmark places for religious worship and other observances in the Government-controlled residential, educational, commercial and industrial complexes.[29] Religion is not discounted at any level, which is perhaps a much more honest and realistic understanding of proper positioning of politics in a conservative society. Jeff Haynes writes, "Secular ideologies, invariably drawn from the developed countries' experiences, including nationalism, socialism, state-building and so on, were tolerated (rarely if ever enthusiastically endorsed) by populations, if two interlinked factors were present. As long as governments were viewed as both authoritative and legitimate, they were accepted (though rarely loved) by their citizens. From the 1970s, however government legitimacy often plummeted in the wake of corruption, economic failure and political repression."[30]

This analysis appears to be more relevant to Nigeria than most of the other countries. For instance, if we see John Hunwick's article on Nigerian politics, we can assume that he has only applied theoretical formulation of Jeff Haynes to the Nigerian case. Hunwick substantiates the theory with

[28] Paden, John (2003), 'Nigeria', in Robert Wuthnow (ed.) "The Encyclopedia of Politics and Religion", Vol. I, p.570, Routledge, London.
[29] "Religion in Nigeria", Wikipedia.
[30] Haynes, Jeff (2003), "Religion in Third World Politics", p.07, Open University Press, Buckingham.

relevant and recent examples from Nigeria. According to him, politicization of religion had two important contributory factors. "The diffusion of political energy and absence of normal political life under military rule" was the first factor." The oil-boom of the mid-1970s followed by the sudden slump in the 1980s" was another factor, "which created discontent and frustration, and Nigerians - both Muslims and Christians - turned to religion, both as refuge and as a political weapon."[31]

Judicial Non-Intervention and Political Resolution of Religious Issues

If we move back to the general (Africa as a whole), after transiting from the general theoretical to the specific (Nigerian case), we will find the same understanding of the problem of religion-politics interface. While Hunwick analyses religion in Nigeria "as a refuge and as a political weapon," Ian Landen's celebrated Commission for Africa Report (prepared for Bob Geldof) evaluates role of religion in Africa "as a language of change and redress." Landen's report appears to be a replication of Jeff Haynes' analysis. According to this Report, "Nationalism in Africa is exhausted and political and state structures have lost all credibility or legitimacy. Into the vacuum left by the failure of nation-state, has stepped religion. Religion has succeeded where the state failed." The Report contrasts Africa with Europe - "A comprehensively dechristianized Europe pretends that faith is simply a personal hobby ... while Africa has experienced an astonishing increase in religiosity.[32]

As Nigeria's decision-makers have intuitively accepted legitimacy of religion in politics, Nigeria's religions have become "public religions," which consider "society as an arena of possible moral good and as desanctified zone of contestation among groups in civil society to forge public policy."[33] The "public" status of religion gives these religions "rightful voice and place in debates in the civil society. It resists moves to force the sheer

---

[31] Hunwick, John, op.cit., p.148-149.
[32] Bunting, Madeiline (2005), "Africa: Where Faith is a Healer", The Guardian, 28 March, http:/www.guardian.co.up/ politics/2005.
[33] Coleman, John A. (2003), "American Catholics, Catholic Charities USA, and Welfare Reform in Religion returns to the public square, edited by Hugh Heclo and Wilfred McClay, John Hopkins University Press, Baltimore.

privatization of the religious voices or denude it of its citizenship right to speak."

Nigeria's judicial system also reinforces this public role of religion. Unlike U.S.A. and India, Nigerian judiciary does not intervene in these typical religion-politics turf wars.[34] Because of this judicial non-interventionism, these disputes are not settled in the cool chambers of civil courts but spill over onto the hot and dusty streets. The grievances are articulated in sporadic and spontaneous acts. It results in violence and disruption of civic life. This is the ugly part of the phenomena. The other consequence is functional to the system. Since religion-in-the-politics category of disputes is not within the purview of courts, they get only political space to contend. We all know that political process involves popular participation, democratic churning, bargaining spirit of give and take, compromises under compulsion and also nightmarish alterative scenario of imminent anarchy, if contending groups fail to settle their disputes through accommodation of other opposing views. The political process, in spite of being dilatory and disintegrative, is ultimately more effective, acceptable and long-standing. Thus political resolution of religious conflict is a better option than the judicial resolution, though political resolution may not be any better than a mere adjustment. Also, since in Nigeria, religion-in-politics issues could be settled only through political processes, political process is always overloaded and overworked. Casual observers may find the penetration of religion in the Nigerian political system, too deep and disturbing but this, as we have seen, is only one aspect of the phenomena at work.

---

[34] John Paden. op.cit. P. 570 "The general practice in Nigeria is not to use legal services in pursuit of fundamental or religious rights. Rather, grievances are addressed through the political process, even when that process is military rather than civilian."

CONTRIBUTORS

SYEDA HAMEED is a distinguished scholar and writer, and prominent women's rights activist. She is currently Member, Planning Commission, Government of India, New Delhi.

PRAKASH KARAT, renowned communist leader, is General Secretary of Communist Party of India (Marxist).

YASHWANT SINHA is a senior Bhartiya Janata Party (BJP) leader and Member of Parliament (Lok Sabha). He served both as Minister of Finance and Minister of Foreign Affairs in the National Democratic Alliance (NDA) Government, at the centre.

SURESH NEOTIA, distinguished industrialist, is the Chairman, Ambuja Cement Foundation, New Delhi.

A.B. BARDHAN is General Secretary of Communist Party of India (CPI).

S. AYYAPPAN is the Director General, Indian Council of Agricultural Research, New Delhi.

C.P. CHANDRASEKHAR is a Professor, Centre for Economic Studies and Planning, School of Social Sciences, Jawaharlal Nehru University (JNU), New Delhi.

SANJAY BARU formerly Media Adviser to Prime Minister of India.

KAMAL NAYAN KABRA is a Political Economist and former Professor of Economics, Indian Institute of Public Administration, New Delhi.

P. L. GAUTAM is the Chairman, National Biodiversity Authority, Chennai.

G. VENKATARAMANI is Expert Consultant, National Biodiversity Authority, Chennai.

AJIT KUMAR SINGH is the Director, Giri Institute of Development Studies, Lucknow.

ASHUTOSH MISHRA is a Reader, Department of Political Science, Lucknow University, Lucknow.

Acknowledgment

We are grateful to the Editorial Advisory Board of Think India Quarterly and all the authors who contributed their articles for the special issue on Indian Economy. We tried to accommodate diverse opinions and outlooks on Indian Economy. This is a humble endeavour to acknowledge the knowledge of economic development in our fast changing country. We are specially thankful to Prof. Pushpesh Pant, Prof. CP Chandrasekhar , Sanjeev Ranjan and Dhananjay Tripathy for their untiring efforts in bringing out the book.

- D. P. Tripathi

New Delhi

Index

www.ingramcontent.com/pod-product-compliance
Lightning Source LLC
Chambersburg PA
CBHW050235270326
41914CB00033BB/1929/J